Morris F. (Morris Francis) 1n Dowley

History and honorary roll of the Twelfth Regiment, Infantry, N.G.S.N.Y.

Morris F. (Morris Francis) 1n Dowley

History and honorary roll of the Twelfth Regiment, Infantry, N.G.S.N.Y.

ISBN/EAN: 9783744738842

Printed in Europe, USA, Canada, Australia, Japan

Cover: Foto ©ninafisch / pixelio.de

More available books at **www.hansebooks.com**

HISTORY AND HONORARY ROLL

OF THE

Twelfth Regiment, Infantry,

N. G. S. N. Y.

Containing a full and accurate account of the various changes through which the organization has passed since the date of its formation (1847) to the present; also biographical sketches of General Butterfield, Ward, and Barlow, and Rev. Stephen H. Tyng, Jr., as well as the names and rank of several hundred members of the "Twelfth" who rose to distinction during the war for the suppression of the Great Rebellion.

BY

M. FRANCIS DOWLEY,
COUNSELOR-AT-LAW,
NEW YORK.

PUBLISHED BY

T. FARRELL & SON,
107 FULTON STREET, NEW YORK.

1 8 6 9.

CONTENTS.

PAGE.

PREFACE.
Introduction.
Organization of the Twelfth Regiment.................1, 2, 3, 4
Order to Consolidate the Twelfth Regiment with the Tenth
    N. Y. S. M.. 6
The Twelfth Regiment Merged in the Twenty-Second......... 11
Departure for Washington, 1861............................ 14
Opinions of the Press..................................... 15
Second Term of Service, 1862.............................. 17
The Twelfth Regiment at Harper's Ferry, 1862.............. 18
Third Term of Service, 1863............................... 22
Report of Inspector General Liebenau, Relative to Present Condition of Twelfth Regiment................................ 23

HONORARY ROLL.

Astor, John J., Lieutenant Colonel........................ 24
Butterfield, Daniel, Major General........................ 25
Barlow, Francis C., "   " 28
Burdett, A., Surgeon...................................... 24
Bendix, John E., Brigadier General........................ 65
Cocks, John S., Colonel................................... 24
Coolidge, F. W., Paymaster................................ 24
Daly, J. T., Rev., First Chaplain......................... 24
French, Richard, Colonel.................................. 24
Locke, F. T., Brevet Brigadier General.................... 34
Satterlee, Livingston, Lieutenant Colonel................. 39

CONTENTS.

Tyng, S. H., Jr., Chaplain............................. 38
Ward, William G., Brigadier General.............. 32
Ward, John, Colonel................................... 36
Present Field and Staff Officers of the Twelfth Regiment....... 42
A Company.. 43
B   " 48
C   " 58
D   " 62
E   " 65
F   " 76
G   " 83
H   " 87
I   " 91
K   " 97
Bill of Dress of the Twelfth Regiment.................... 101
Extracts from the Military Code of the State of New York.... 113
Drills and Parades 146
Compensation for Military Service....................... 156
Regimental and Battalion Courts-Martial.................. 164
Fines and Penalties.................................... 166
Miscellaneous Provisions............................... 188
Addenda.

PREFACE.

The officers, members and admirers of the "Twelfth Regiment" have long desired to see in print its "History and Honorary Roll." Its compilation being a work requiring no small amount of application and research, several shrunk from its performance.

I have culled the materials for this volume from many a mass of old orders, private manuscripts and inspection returns, during the leisure hours allowed by my clients and professional duties.

Owing to the scattered condition of the necessary matter, I frequently thought that it would be said of me as of those who previously attempted the work : "*Hic homo cepit edificare et non potuit consummare.*" Still, I persevered and the following pages are the fruits of my perseverance.

That the labor could have been more successfully performed by other hands, I know, but not, I believe, by any who could have sought more earnestly to do it well. And if the parties for whom this book is compiled find even a small degree of pleasure and satisfaction in its perusal, I shall deem my efforts amply rewarded. Of those who may criticise, I only ask them to remember that :

"Whoever thinks a faultless piece to see,
Thinks what ne'er was, nor is, nor e'er shall be."

M. F. D.

INTRODUCTION.

The Twelfth Regiment being a Militia organization, I deem it apropos to present here facts and figures to show the importance and necessity of a well-organized Militia force. Our volunteer troops are, by many, depreciated, simply because they are not aware of the invaluable services rendered by said troops to the State and National Governments.

Owing to the admirable manner in which this subject was presented to the New York Constitutional Convention, by Brig. Gen. Selden E. Marvin, Adjutant General of the State, I take the liberty of quoting the following extracts from his article :

"In our State the Militia has been sustained and kept up for more than a half a century and while it has had much opposition at times strewn in its way, it has continued to prosper and its fruits have been apparent in the manner in which it has at all times and under all circumstances and in all emergencies, discharged its duties.

"Prior to the late terrible conflict, very many of the people of the State looked upon the existence of the Militia with eyes of disrespect and laughed at the efforts that were being made for its support, pouring out invectives of contumely and contempt and, like many of the most important institutions of society and government, the inestimable importance of a well-organized Militia was ignored by the great mass and it was only in the consideration of its entire abolition, or in the exercise of its fullest authority and influence in the hour of need, that its indispensable functions were recognized and appreciated. So much opposition was engendered, that those who saw clearly the necessity of maintaining the organization, found many obstacles to encounter and difficulties to overcome, much self-sacrifice was demanded and the reproaches of the many well-nigh stifled the efforts of the few. But manfully and heroically the battle was fought, the war came and the labor of years was crowned with success.

"The importance of the Militia as a strictly military force can not be too highly estimated. It constitutes the true military strength of the republic, in which the people retain all the power, as in its co-ordinate branch, the civil authority. It is organized in accordance with the spirit of the Constitution of the United States and is made applicable to the condition of the country in its growing capacity and extended relations. Its governance is under constitutions and laws prescribed and regulated by the people and for the support of the Government created by and sustained for the people.

"In a time when taxation is grievous and falls with heaviness upon the people, the Militia, in its relations to political economy, is of the greatest importance. The cost of the maintenance of the entire force of the National Guard in this State in a high state of efficiency, would not support a single regiment of the Regular Army, including all contingent expenses and yet, as has been proved, the Militia would be as serviceable as the forces whose business is war.

"And again, the National Guard, as an auxiliary to the Police Force of the State is indispensable. It is the only reliance the people have in the suppression of riots and the wiping out of local insurrections. To think of maintaining a constabulary force for such emergencies would be absurd. The cost for a force sufficiently large for all such emergencies, especially in large centres of population, would be immense and insupportable.

"The Militia, in its well-conceived organization and with liberal support, exerts a moral influence upon the evil-disposed and thereby prevents the inception of plots or designs of organized resistance to the laws. It is, in times of such danger, the sole resource of the people and gives to legislative and judicial decisions their force and influence. Without such a reliable resource it is possible and even probable, that laws and the decisions and verdicts of constituted authorities, would be nugatory and despised. A small proportion of the people, if evil disposed, could, by concerted and well-organized action, defy the large majority of peaceable and law-abiding citizens. Such a successful resistance of law, if even for a very limited period, would demoralize society and the loss of life inevitable in such collisions would be terrible and the value of the property which might be jeoparded would support an adequate Militia for centuries.

"In this connection, permit me to furnish a brief *resumé* of the services of the National Guard.

"Whenever it has been necessary in various localities to call upon the military authorities for aid and support, the response has always been attended with promptness and the service effectually performed. The Police Force has always found in the Military a sure and reliable body for its support and it has ever proved effective in the suppression of riots and in upholding the civil form of government. In the Astor Place riots, the police difficulties, the bread riots of 1857, the Quarantine riots and the antirent troubles, the Militia has ever faithfully discharged all duties imposed upon them by the civil authorities. In the late war its services have been largely felt and its influences have been spread over a large extent of the success that attended our armies.

"A brief synopsis of the service in the late war, I trust, will not be regarded as tedious or out of place.

"In April, 1861, immediately after the rebellion had been actively inaugurated and the safety of the National Capitol was threatened, the State of New York furnished and forwarded to the points of danger eleven regiments, comprising 7,334 officers and men, whose presence undoubtedly saved the nation from a great and almost fatal calamity at the very outbreak of actual hostilities. That the State, after so long a period of profound peace, should have been enabled to promptly furnish this force for the National exigency, is a marked and undeniable indication of the natural and innate martial spirit of its citizens. This martial spirit nobly evinced during the great revolution and rekindled during the war of 1812, has never been quenched in this State and ever since this last-named epoch, a military organization more or less efficient has been sustained under exclusive State influences and authority, without assistance or encouragement from the General Government and during long years of peace, when the martial profession was deemed the most useless office of man, the New York Militia, at its own expense and despite every discouragement, retained that organization and schooled officers and soldiers for the nation's greatest need.

"In addition to the force above-named, six complete regiments of the State Militia volunteered during the first months of the war and were mustered into the service for and served three years. Over five thousand officers for Volunteer regiments were furnished by the Militia of the State.

"The rebellion having revived in all a military ardor and the advance in military science and the unexpected draft upon the national resources having exhibited defects and suggested their remedies, the Legislature of the State, after consideration, enacted, April 23, 1862, an amended law, which provided for the enrollment of the arms-bearing population and the organization of an active force, entitled the 'National Guard,' with a maximum since fixed at 50,000 men. While this body was in process of organization, the State was enabled to furnish, from its incomplete ranks, twelve regiments, comprising 8,588 men, who were mustered into the United States service for three months, in May, 1862; and again, after the active volunteering and drafts for the general service had depleted their ranks, twenty-six regiments, comprising 13,971 men, marched, in 1863, to the defense of Pennsylvania and Maryland. Again, in 1864, ten regiments of the National Guard were mustered into the United States service for one hundred days. During the years of 1864 and 1865, when threatened raids from Canada harassed and distracted the Government, the National Guard, ordered on duty at exposed points of the frontier, relieved the apprehensions of our citizens, saved the detaching of troops from the armies in front of Richmond, and frustrated the designs of our enemies.

"This hasty sketch of the service of the Militia of this State displays their efficiency and usefulness at a period when the demands of the General Government, by volunteering or forced drafts from their ranks, constantly tended to impair and disorganize them and exhibits a vitality and zeal under every discouragement, which deserves and should receive the respect and consideration of all.

"After the close of the war had returned to the State its hundreds of thousands of veterans, scarred on every great battle-field, the organization of the National Guard was resumed and completed, until it now comprises one hundred and ten regiments of infantry, artillery and cavalry and fifty-two thousand officers and men, most of them armed, uniformed and equipped in the most complete manner; an army of disciplined citizens, representing every class of society; intelligent, brave and ardent, bound by every relation of life to sustain social and political order and prepared at a moment's notice to vindicate the enforcement of the laws, National or State, or repel invasions from abroad."

Active membership in a regiment like the Twelfth, may be made a physical and moral school for young men, developing in them qualities which commerce, trades and civil professions dwarf or destroy. The exercise is healthy, manly and inspiring. The discipline is calculated to make men obedient, punctual and moral. And when the Legislature of New York shall have passed a law, making the term of service in the National Guard *four* instead of *seven* years; allowing members of the National Guard going to or returning from drills, parades, or encampments, to ride *free* on ferries, steam and street cars; then recruits in abundance will be obtained, by exciting the military instincts which characterize the healthy young men of our State. Recruits thus obtained, are worth ten times as much as those who are "danced into a regiment at military balls" and whose conception of National Guardsmen is limited to showy uniforms, brass buttons and fascinations to the gay belles of fashion.

The Twelfth Regiment has no recruits of the latter character. But its ranks are filled by spirited young men, who do duty through patriotic motives, notwithstanding the personal inconvenience and expense which the present Militia Law imposes on members of the National Guard. Let the Legislature, at its next session, enact that the term of service shall be shortened and that officers and members of the National Guard shall enjoy the other privileges aforesaid, and results will follow; pleasant to every enlisted man and beneficial to the State.

M. F. D.

HISTORY

OF THE

TWELFTH REGIMENT, INFANTRY.

N. G. S. N. Y.

CHAPTER FIRST.

THE TWELFTH REGIMENT was organized on the 6th of May, 1847. It originated in the blending of the following flank companies:

Light Guard, now Company A, Capt. Vincent.
City Musketeers, do. B, do. Palmer.
Tompkins Blues, do. C, do. Besson.
City Blues, do. D, do. Johnson.
Guard Lafayette, do. E, do. Leclerc.
Lafayette Fusileers, do. F, do. French.
Independence Guard, do. G, do. Cairns.
Baxter Blues, do. H, do. Waterbury.
Baxter Guard, do. I, do. Dyckman.
New York Riflemen, do. L, do. Johnson.

The Field and Staff Officers of the Regiment at its formation were:

Colonel, Henry G. Stebbins.
Lieutenant Colonel, John J. Astor, subsequently E. B. Hart.
Adjutant, J. B. Stearns.
Paymaster, F. W. Coolidge.
Quartermaster, T. C. Fields.
Surgeon, A. Burdett.
Engineer, J. Livingston.
Chaplain, J. T. Daly.

For two years each of the aforesaid companies wore its distinctive uniform. In 1849 they adopted as the regimental uniform a plain fatigue cap and jacket. The Regiment turned out for duty in this dress during the Astor Place riots.

The officer at that time commanding the Twelfth, in Order No. 5, speaks thus of the Regiment's conduct during said riots :

"The promptness exhibited by the several companies, in compliance with an order of scarcely two hours' notice, to assemble on the 16th and 17th insts., to aid in the suppression of a riot then threatening the peace of our city, reflects the highest honor upon both officers and men. The Colonel can not let the occasion pass without expressing his entire satisfaction of the manner in which the orders to assemble, on both of those days, were obeyed ; and the gratification which his command afforded him by the soldier-like deportment manifested while under arms, during a time of so much public excitement. He trusts that there may never again be a necessity for calling upon the Regiment for such unpleasant duty."

In 1853 the Regiment laid aside the plain fatigue cap and jacket, and adopted a most showy and attractive uniform, the famous part of which was the white coat. In these gay regimentals, the Twelfth turned out, 400 strong, to celebrate the opening of the Crystal Palace ; but the parade on Evacuation Day, November 25, 1854, surpassed the latter display in numbers and brilliancy.

The following, from the *Military Argus* of December 21, 1854, relating to the parade on the 25th of November of the last-named year, may be interesting :

The great feature of the day was the Twelfth Regiment, Col. Stebbins, between which and the Seventh a rivalry honorable to both exists. Upon this occasion the Twelfth had decidedly the advantage in numbers, and in fact their marching and wheeling, as well as the manual of arms, was in every respect equal to the National Guard. The following table will show distinctly the relative force of the two Regiments on this day, omitting, of course, the National Guard Troop, which rarely parades with the Regiment.

TWELFTH REGIMENT, COL. STEBBINS.

Field, Line, and Staff	35
Corps of Engineers, Lieut. Hubbard	18
Company A, Light Guard, Capt. Vincent	69
do. I, Baxter Guard, Capt. Dyckman	32
do. C, Tompkins Blues, Capt. Besson	32
do. H, Baxter Blues, Capt. Waterbury	56
do. F, Lafayette Fusileers, Capt. McCauly	28
do. D, City Blues, Capt. Fowler	50
do. B, Washington Light Guard, Capt. Thomas	26
do. G, Independence Guard, Lieut. Boyle	35
do. L, Black Rifles, Capt. Johnson	94
Pioneer and Sword Guard	11
do. E, Guard Lafayette and 11 Pioneers	124
Total	610

SEVENTH REGIMENT, COL. DURYEA.

Field, Line, and Staff	36
Eight Companies, averaging 36 men each	288
Total	324

The above shows that Col. Stebbins paraded 286 more men than Col. Duryea, a most important difference.

The Twelfth seemed now destined to become the most celebrated regiment in the Union. But all things human are uncertain and mutable. In 1855 the Regiment began to decline, and the future, that appeared so bright, grew dark. This sudden and unfavorable change in the Regiment's condition and prospects was occasioned by the resignation of its noble commandant, Henry G. Stebbins.

Shortly after the resignation of Col. Stebbins, Richard French, the courteous proprietor of the well-known hotel of the same name, assumed command, the field officers being Col. French, Lieut. Col. Hart, and Maj. Stearns. The famous white coats were now discarded, and a new uniform, consisting of a blue coat, white pantaloons, etc., adopted. In pursuance of Brigade Orders, this Regiment paraded, under Col. French, on the 4th of June, 1856. Toward the close of the last-named year, Col. French resigned, and Lieut. Col. Stearns assumed command. But he, too, soon withdrew from the organization.

On the 25th of April, 1857, the following officers were chosen:

  Colonel, John S. Cocks.
  Lieutenant Colonel, Henry A. Weeks.
  Major, William Watts.

Under command of these new officers, a battalion drill took place on the afternoon of May 20, 1857, at Hamilton Square. Companies A, B, C, D, G, H, and a flank rifle company were present, making a total of 209.

CHAPTER SECOND.

On Monday, the 14th day of September, 1857, this Regiment paraded in full uniform, white pants, as an escort to the First Regiment New York Volunteers (a large portion of whose officers were furnished by the Twelfth), took part in the reception of the "Scott Legion," of Pennsylvania, companions in arms during the war with Mexico, and subsequently joined in celebrating the glorious anniversary of the surrender of the city of Mexico to the American Army.

The rank and file of the Twelfth, inspected in October, 1857, numbered only 136. But in the following month, a slight augmentation was perceptible at the Division Parade. The Regiment continued to drill with five companies till the 23d of April, 1858. At this time, Capt. Helme's Continentals, numbering twenty-five men, were transferred from the Eleventh, and became I Company in the Twelfth Regiment.

Col. Cocks, in Special Orders No. 5, speaks of the Continentals' transfer as follows: "Capt. John C. Helme, having reported himself and command for duty, in compliance with General Orders No. 41, transferring said Captain and company, in accordance with their expressed desire, from the Eleventh Regiment to this, he and his command are received by the Twelfth Regiment with a soldier's welcome."

Immediately after the Continentals joining the Regiment, Col. Cocks, in regard to the removal of Company L from the Twelfth, speaks thus in the aforesaid Order: "It is with sincere regret that the Colonel is obliged to announce the transfer of Company L, which he regards as a very considerable loss to the Regiment, and more particularly that of Capt. Louis Heitkamp, whose officer-like and gentlemanly deportment at all times, together with his ability and strict attention to duty, has secured for him the highest respect of his brother officers, and especially that of his Colonel. In thus parting with Company L, the best wishes of the Twelfth Regiment go with the Captain and his command."

At the date of the transfer of the aforementioned companies, the Regiment laid aside the old flint style for the superior percussion lock. The Engineer Corps took the vacant letter A, and formed a company under command of Capt. George H. Barr.

On account of the Regiment's non-appearance on parade when the remains of ex-President Monroe passed through this city for Richmond (July 3, 1858), Col. Cocks, on a false charge of disobedience of orders, was placed under arrest. This abuse of power reflects no credit on the parties who ordered said arrest. It was the first of several acts bearing the marks of official enmity which were exercised toward Col. Cocks and his Regiment. Parties in New York and Albany, by misrepresentations, obtained from the State General Headquarters, an Order to consolidate the Twelfth with the Tenth New York State Militia, under Col. Halsey. Owing to the peculiarity and importance of said Order, it is given here in full, to recall to the memories of the members of the Twelfth Regiment reminiscences of bygone days, which, though at the time of their occurrence occasioned a frown, can now but awaken a smile.

GENERAL HEADQUARTERS, STATE OF NEW YORK.

SPECIAL ORDERS No. 56.

ADJUTANT GENERAL'S OFFICE,
ALBANY, *March* 16, 1859.

I.—The Commander-in-Chief has had under consideration a recommendation for the consolidation of the Tenth and Twelfth Regiments of the Fourth Brigade, contained in the following communication from Maj. Gen. Charles W. Sandford, of the First Division, and Brig. Gen. John Ewen, of the Fourth Brigade:

"HEADQUARTERS FIRST DIVISION N. Y. S. M.,
NEW YORK, *February* 21, 1859.

"*To the Commander-in-Chief of the State of New York:*

"The undersigned, Commandants of the First Division and of the Fourth Brigade, New York State Militia, respectfully represent that the Tenth and Twelfth Regiments, Fourth Brigade, N. Y. S. M., having at the two last annual inspections fallen in numerical strength much below the standard required by our laws and the good of the service, they recommend that said regiments be consolidated; and for this purpose they would propose that Companies A and C of the Twelfth Regiment be consolidated together; that Companies B and H of the same regiment be consolidated together; that Companies G and F of the same regiment be consolidated together; and that the companies so consolidated, with Company D of the same regiment, be transferred to and consolidated with the Tenth Regiment, under the command of Col. Halsey. And the undersigned further recommend that Company F of the Tenth Regiment be transferred to the Eleventh Regiment, Col. Bostwick. All which is respectfully submitted.

"CHAS. W. SANDFORD, *Maj. Gen. First Division.*
"JOHN EWEN, *Brig. Gen. Fourth Brigade.*"

II.—The Commander-in-Chief coincides with Gens. Sandford and Ewen in the propriety of the consolidation, and is pleased to direct that it be effected in the manner proposed in their communication.

III.—To this end it is hereby ordered that Companies A and C of the Twelfth Regiment be consolidated together; that Companies B and H of the same regiment be consolidated together; that Companies G and E of the same regiment be consolidated together; that the companies so consolidated, with Company D of the same regiment, be transferred to and consolidated with the Tenth Regiment, under the command of Col. William Halsey; and that Company F of the Tenth Regiment be transferred to the Eleventh Regiment, same Brigade.

IV.—Gen. Ewen will superintend the consolidation hereby ordered, and will, as soon as it is effected, direct the several commandants of companies thus consolidated or transferred to report for duty to the commandants of the regiments to which they are transferred.

V.—After the consolidation has been completely effected, Col. William Halsey, commanding the Tenth Regiment, will transmit to these Headquarters a roster of his regiment, giving the letters of companies, the names of their officers, and the number of non-commissioned officers and privates therein respectively.

VI.—All officers rendered supernumerary by the provisions of this order will report to this office.

By order of the Commander-in-Chief.

FRED'K TOWNSEND, *Adj. Gen.*

HEADQUARTERS FIRST DIVISION, N. Y. S. M.

SPECIAL ORDERS No. 3.

NEW YORK, *March* 18, 1859.

The foregoing Special Orders No. 56 are promulgated.

Brig. Gen. Ewen will issue the necessary orders to carry the consolidation into effect, and will make report to the Adjutant General and Major General as soon as the consolidation is completed.

By order of

CHARLES W. SANDFORD, *Maj. Gen.*

R. C. WETMORE, *Division Inspector.*

HEADQUARTERS FOURTH BRIGADE, FIRST DIVISION, N. Y. S. M.

SPECIAL ORDERS No. 4.

NEW YORK, *May* 24, 1859.

I.—The suspension of the promulgation of Special Orders No. 3 to the Twelfth Regiment, pursuant to a writ of alternative mandamus from the Supreme Court, since annulled, having rendered modifications therein expedient, it is ordered that these Special Orders be, and the same are hereby, substituted therefor, so far as that Regiment is concerned.

II.—Special Orders No. 56 from General Headquarters, and Special Orders No. 3 from Division Headquarters, are hereby promulgated.

III.—Pursuant to said Orders, it is hereby ordered that Companies A and C of the Twelfth Regiment be consolidated together, under the command of Capt. George H. Barr, the senior Captain, and transferred to and consolidated with the Tenth Regiment, and designated as Company A of said Regiment; that Companies B and H of the

Twelfth Regiment be consolidated together, under the command of Capt. Wm. Huson, the senior Captain, and transferred to and consolidated with the Tenth Regiment, and designated as Company H of said Regiment; that Companies G and E of the Twelfth Regiment be consolidated together, under the command of Capt. James A. Boyle, the senior Captain, and transferred to and consolidated with the Tenth Regiment, and designated as Company F of said Regiment; that Company D of the Twelfth Regiment, commanded by Capt. John D. Ottiwell, be transferred to and consolidated with the Tenth Regiment, and designated as Company D of said Regiment; and that Company F of the Tenth Regiment, commanded by Capt. Henry L. Klein, be transferred to the Eleventh Regiment, and designated as Company G of said Regiment.

IV.—Capt. Henry E. Gotleib, commanding Company C of the Twelfth Regiment, will, on or by Monday, the 30th day of May instant, cause a copy of these and Regimental Orders, and also Company Orders directing members to report without delay to Capt. George H. Barr for duty, to be served upon the members of his Company, and cause a copy of said Orders, with a return of service thereof, to be served upon the Commandant of this Brigade, and also upon Capt. Barr, on or by Wednesday, the 1st day of June next. He will also at such time furnish Capt. Barr with the roll of the members of his company, with their places of residence.

V.—Capt. Garret H. Dyckman, commanding Company H of said Regiment, will, on or by Monday, the 30th day of May instant, cause a copy of these and Regimental Orders, and also Company Orders directing members to report without delay to Capt. Wm. Huson for duty, to be served upon the members of his Company, and cause a copy of such Orders, with a return of service thereof, to be served upon the Commandant of this Brigade, and also upon Capt. Huson, on or by Wednesday, the 1st day of June next. He will also at such time furnish Capt. Huson with the roll of his company, with the places of residence of the members.

VI.—Capt. Higbie Carpenter, commanding Company F of said Regiment, will, on or by Monday, the 30th day of May instant, cause a copy of these Orders, and Company Orders directing the members of his company to report without delay for duty to Capt. James A. Boyle, to be served upon the members of his company, and cause a copy of such Orders, with a return of service thereof, to be served upon the Commandant of this Brigade, and also upon Capt. Boyle, on or by Wednesday, the 1st day of June next. He will at such time furnish to Capt. Boyle the roll of the members of his company, with their places of residence.

VII.—As soon as the duty directed by the IV., V., and VI. paragraphs of these Orders shall be performed, the consolidation of the several companies referred to in paragraph II. shall be considered effected.

TWELFTH REGIMENT. 9

VIII.—Capts. Boyle, Huson, Barr, and Ottiwell will, on or by Friday, the 3d day of June next, report to Col. Wm. Halsey, of the Tenth Regiment, for duty, and at such time furnish him with a copy of a corrected roll of their respective companies, with the places of residence of the members.

IX.—The senior officers in the respective grades of the companies consolidated together and transferred to the Tenth Regiment, are continued in command; the junior officers in such grades are rendered supernumerary.

X.—The officers of such companies will be as follows, viz. :

Company F, Tenth Regiment—Captain, James A. Boyle.
"   "   "   First Lieutenant, Fred. T. Locke.
"   "   "   Second Lieutenant, Charles Cadlip.
"   H,   "   Captain, Wm. Huson.
"   "   "   First Lieutenant, John N. Dixon.
"   "   "   Second Lieutenant, Wm. Gee.
"   A,   "   Captain, Geo. H. Barr.
"   "   "   First Lieutenant, Henry W. Ryder.
"   "   "   Second Lieutenant, John Quincy Adams.

XI.—Lieut. Col. Henry A. Weeks, commanding the Twelfth Regiment, will cause these Orders to be promulgated to the commissioned officers of his command, on or by Friday, the 27th day of May instant, and will furnish to the Commandant of the Brigade a copy of the Orders so promulgated, with a return of service thereof, on or by Monday, the 30th day of May instant.

XII.—Brigade Major Taylor will cause to be supplied to Lieut. Col. Weeks a sufficient number of these General Division and Brigade Orders, with blank Regimental Orders, for promulgation to his command, and will also cause to be supplied to Capts. Gotleib, Dyckman, and Carpenter a sufficient number of the Brigade Orders, with blank Company Orders, for promulgation to their commands.

XIII.—After the consolidation has been completely effected, Col. William Halsey, commanding the Tenth Regiment, will transmit to General and Brigade Headquarters, respectively, a roster of his regiment, giving the letters of companies, the names of their officers, and the number of non-commissioned officers and privates therein respectively.

All officers rendered supernumerary by the provisions of Special Orders No. 53, from General Headquarters, hereby promulgated, will report to the Adjutant General.

By order of

JOHN EWEN, *Brig. Gen. Commanding.*

ROBERT TAYLOR, *Brigade Major and Inspector.*

HISTORY OF THE

HEADQUARTERS TWELFTH REGIMENT, N. Y. S. M.

GENERAL ORDERS No. —.

NEW YORK, *May* 27, 1859.

The foregoing Special Orders from General, Division, and Brigade Headquarters, are hereby promulgated for the information and guidance of this Regiment.

By order of
/ HENRY A. WEEKS, *Lieut. Col. Commanding.*
W. G. WARD, *Adjutant.*
EDWARD M. FISHER, *Serg. Major.*

But with characteristic alacrity and love of justice, the Twelfth, immediately after the issuing of the aforementioned Order, resolved to go to Albany and show the Governor and his staff that the charges preferred against the Regiment were entirely devoid of truth. Therefore, with an excellent band and 226 officers and men, it visited the State Capital, and received the plaudits of the people and the honors of the military; but the looks of State officials were cold, and the visit of the Twelfth (in their opinion) savored of insubordination. Not receiving the treatment and redress which it expected and merited, the Twelfth, on its return, drilled regularly, but refused to report for duty to Col. Halsey, preferring disbandment to degradation.

On the 20th of July, 1859, it paraded for the last time as the "Old Twelfth." Accompanied by an admiring multitude, it proceeded to the State Arsenal in Brooklyn, and there delivered its arms and equipments.

Chagrined, but not disheartened, the command returned to New York, and experienced from all classes sympathy and respect. Though broken by the false representations of envious parties, the Twelfth had in it a lustre that could never decay. The regimental organization was still kept up, and the following order issued :

HEADQUARTERS INDEPENDENCE GUARD, TWELFTH REGIMENT, N. Y. S. M.

NEW YORK, 1859.

ORDER }
No. 3. }

This Regiment will assemble in fatigue dress, for Battalion Drill, at the Division Armory, on Wednesday, the 24th inst., at 7½ o'clock P.M.

In accordance with the unanimous decision of the Board of Officers, the Regiment will hereafter be designated, in connection with its numerical distinction, as the INDEPENDENCE GUARD—a name commemorative of our earliest national existence, suggestive of our rights and privileges as citizens, and a worthy stimulant to such exertion as shall reflect lustre both on it and ourselves.

In making this announcement, your Commandant acknowledges the pleasure and satisfaction derived from such an exhibition of unanimity of feeling and interest, as shown by the relinquishment of company distinctions; and is thereby fully convinced, that all individual preferences, or company prejudices, have yielded to a mutual determination that the future success and prosperity of the Regiment shall be the prominent object of our exertions.

By order of

COL. J. S. COCKS,

W. G. WARD, *Adj't Twelfth Regiment.*

EDMD. W. FISHER, *Sergeant Major.*

On the 16th of November, 1859, a new organization was effected, and an order issued from General Headquarters creating five companies, and assigning them to the Twenty-Second Regiment. Immediately thereafter Col. Cocks resigned.

The companies assigned as above retained the title of "Independence Guard," and the Twelfth was thus for a time merged in the Twenty-Second. About the period of this numerical change the following officers were chosen:

Col. (now Brevet Major General U. S. A.) Daniel Butterfield; Lieut. Col. Henry A. Weeks. The first Order issued by Col. Butterfield to his new command read thus:

HEADQUARTERS INDEPENDENCE GUARD, TWENTY-SECOND REGIMENT, N. Y. S. M.

NEW YORK, *December* 7, 1859.

GENERAL ORDERS, }
No. 1. }

The officers and non-commissioned officers of this Regiment are hereby ordered to assemble for drill at the Mercer House, on Wednesday, December 14th, at 7¾ P. M. Fatigue Dress—Overcoat.

The Regiment will assemble for drill at the Division Armory, White Street, on Monday, December 19th, at 7¾ P. M.

Fatigue Dress—Overcoat and Body Belt, without arms. The drills will not be public.

At the first regular meeting of the Board of Officers, the Bill of Dress and By-Laws of the former organization, Independence Guard, were unanimously adopted until otherwise ordered by the Board.

The officers and non-commissioned officers are expected to be thoroughly familiar with the first thirty pages, Vol. I. Scott's Tactics, and ready to answer any questions in regard to same previous to the drill above ordered.

Col. BUTTERFIELD will attend at the Division Board Room, White Street, on Monday, December 12th, from 3½ to 5 P. M. for the purpose of issuing warrants to, and examination of, the non-commissioned officers.

Commandants of companies are requested to make returns of the elections for Sergeants on or before that time, and to furnish the Adjutant with a complete roster of their companies, giving residence and place of business of every member.

The attention of officers is called to the following paragraphs in the book of "General Regulations," viz., 43–454 to 498–525–526.

STAFF APPOINTMENTS.

Henry A. Bostwick, Adjutant.
Henry Slack, Surgeon.
Albert H. Nicolay, Quartermaster.
Richard S. Palmer, Paymaster.

Francis H. Saltus, Ordnance Officer.
Theo. Timpson, Ass't Engineer, (Acting Engineer.)

By order of
COL. DANIEL BUTTERFIELD.
HENRY A. BOSTWICK, *Adjutant.*

It soon became apparent that the aforesaid numerical change was detrimental to the organization. Hence, Col. Butterfield petitioned the Commander-in-chief to restore the old and acceptable number Twelve.

The wished-for numerical restoration took place on or about the first of January, 1860. The command again paraded eight full companies, as the Twelfth Regiment, N. Y. S. M., on Washington's Birthday, 1860. For the Twelfth and its friends, that was a joyous and triumphal parade.

In the following Spring and Summer a system of morning drills was successfully introduced, which proved beneficial in a physical as well as in a military point of view. Lieut. Col. Weeks resigned in September of the aforesaid year.

In pursuance of Division and Brigade Orders, this Regiment assembled for parade, in full uniform, on Thursday, October 11, 1860, at the reception of the Prince of Wales. Maj. Gen. Sandford conferred upon this command the honor of receiving the Prince, and escorting him to position in line. In the course of the same month (October) the Regiment proceeded to Staten Island for target practice.

On the 25th of the following November, Col. Butterfield awarded prizes and medals to the best marksmen in the Regiment, at Madison Square. Toward the close of the same year, the Regiment assembled in full uniform—blue trowsers, white gloves, and white pompon, with fatigue caps slung, and proceeded to Staten Island for field drill. On their return to the city, the command received and escorted to their quarters the Fifth Regiment, Col. Schwarzwaelder, on their return from Bedloe's Island.

CHAPTER THIRD.

WHEN Southern traitors threatened riot and rebellion should Abraham Lincoln proceed to Washington for inauguration, the services of the Twelfth were secretly offered to the Government. The whole command made arrangements to accompany the President elect, in citizen's dress, to rendezvous at a certain point, where they would be furnished with arms and equipments. Said plans and details were submitted to and approved by Lieut. Gen. Winfield Scott.

The Twelfth alone can claim the honor of having been the first regiment which offered its services for the suppression of rebellion. Immediately after inauguration, Col. Butterfield and his officers held several meetings to devise means and adopt measures for placing the command in efficient condition.

On the night of the bombardment of Fort Sumter, the Regiment adopted the chasseur uniform. Its ranks were filled to the maximum standard, and its services tendered to the Government.

Accordingly, the command, numbering nine companies, left New York for Washington, on the 21st day of April, 1861. There were 650 *raw recruits*, in addition to said companies. The Baltic (the steamship in which the Regiment sailed) cleared for Fortress Monroe, but instead of going up the Potomac, the vessel was ordered to Annapolis, by Gen. Butler. After landing and taking a brief repose, the Regiment started for the Junction. On the following Sunday the Twelfth reached Washington, and without delay built wooden huts in Franklin Square.

On the 2d of May, 1861, Major, afterward Gen. McDowell, mustered the command for three months into the United States service. The drill and discipline of Camp Anderson, as the camping ground was styled, were admirable and rigid. Hence, the Twelfth, whilst there, were frequently called *Regulars*.

On the 23d of May, 1861, the Regiment crossed the famous Long Bridge, and was the first Union regiment that set foot on the sacred soil of the " Old Dominion." Its station was at Roach's Mills, at that time the most exposed position.

"The position of the Federal troops around Washington has experienced no material change, with the exception of the return of the Seventy-First to their old quarters at the Navy Yard. The Twelfth New York Regiment may be said to take the post of honor, being the first to cross Long Bridge, and the first to receive an attack after the army of the invasion crossed into Virginia."—*New York Herald*, 1861.

"Col. Butterfield's Twelfth Regiment, which has its location on the heights toward Arlington, is in equally good condition, and anxious for an early contest with its country's assailants. The Twelfth was justly and highly honored by Gen. Mansfield in being given the lead in the movement of Thursday night. It was the first regiment to enter Virginia, and if needs be will be the last to leave it. In ten minutes from the time the order was given on Thursday evening, the men were out of their beds, dressed and in marching order, and so quietly did they leave their city encampment, that the residents in the city were not aware of their departure until the following day. In all that pertains to strict discipline, accurate drill, and soldierly bearing, the Twelfth Regiment is unsurpassed, and an honor to its accomplished Colonel."—*New York Post*, 1861.

"An incident came to our knowledge a few days since which we take pleasure in giving place to, inasmuch as it exemplifies the old adage, 'One good turn deserves another,' and shows the cordial soldierly feeling which exists among the military.

"In the Summer of 1859 the Twelfth Regiment were ordered by the Major General commanding the First Division to deliver up their arms. The order caused much ill-feeling among the members of the Regiment, but it was obeyed. On marching to the Brooklyn Arsenal, which was the place assigned for the custody of the muskets, the Regiment were reviewed by the Mayor and Aldermen Dayton and Van Brunt, of Brooklyn, who also extended other courtesies to the Regiment.

"On the arrival of the Fourteenth Regiment in Washington last week, the corps was but insufficiently provided with music. Alderman Dayton was at the capital, and desiring that the Brooklyn boys should make a fine appearance on marching up Pennsylvania Avenue, knowing full well that music was a necessary adjunct, proceeded to the camp of the Twelfth Regiment, and inquired for Col. Butterfield. That gentlemen was not present, but Lieut. Col. Ward was sent for.

Alderman Dayton briefly explained the position of the Fourteenth, and Lieut. Col. Ward, remembering the kindness of the Alderman three years before, ordered the regimental band to proceed to the depot and play for the Brooklyn boys. The band went down to the depot on a double quick march. The regiment was all formed, the band took up their position, and the Fourteenth marched up the avenue the observed of all observers, making a decidedly brilliant appearance."—*New York Post*, 1861.

On the 2d of the following June the Twelfth returned to Washington, and on the 7th of July was ordered to Hagerstown. The command had now been recruited to the grand number of 1,023. After bivouacking in Hagerstown Woods, it moved to Williamsport, forded the Potomac, marched all night, and arrived at Martinsburg on the 9th, just at the dawn of the morning.

About this time Col. Butterfield was appointed acting Brigadier General. The Fifth, Twelfth, Nineteenth, and Twenty-Eighth New York Volunteers comprising his command.

On the 15th of July the Twelfth moved to Camp Patterson, at Bunkers Hill, Md.; thence, on the 17th, to Camp McClellan, at Charlestown, and on the following Sunday proceeded to Harper's Ferry, and occupied a position on Bolivar Heights. Afterward they passed to the ground near the Indiana Zouaves, and called the same Camp Butterfield. Then the services of the Regiment were tendered to and accepted by the War Department.

On the 26th of July, 1861, Companies A, B, C, and E crossed the Shenandoah, and took possession of the block-houses built by the rebels on Loudon Heights. There they remained till after the evacuation of Harper's Ferry by Gen. Banks. They were the last troops to cross the Potomac, and had to ford two rivers before rejoining the army.

On the 28th of July the Regiment was forwarded to Knoxville, Md.; thence ordered to New York, where it arrived on Friday evening, August 2, 1861, and received a grand and flattering welcome.

CHAPTER FOURTH.

THE New York troops were called out on the 27th of May, 1862, for a second term of three months' service. The Twelfth at once volunteered. After some delay in procuring uniforms, arms, and equipments, it departed for Baltimore.

Company A was ordered to drill in Fort McHenry, and the balance of the Regiment sent to Harper's Ferry. Here a brigade was formed by the Twelfth and Twenty-Second New York, and the Eighty-Seventh Ohio. The Twelfth encamped near the neat village of Bolivar, on the heights overlooking the Potomac.

The daily routine was as follows:

Reveille at sunrise.
Surgeon's call, 5.30 A. M.
Drill, 6 till 7.30 A. M.
Guard mounting, 8 A. M.
Company drill, 9 till 10.30 A. M.
First Sergeant's call, 12 M.
Roast beef, 1 P. M.
Fatigue, 2 P. M.
Battalion drill, 4.45 till 6.45 P. M.
Tattoo at 9 P. M.

SUNDAY MORNINGS.

Inspection at 8.30 A. M.
Religious services at 10.30 A. M.

The Regiment having a large number of inexperienced recruits, required incessant drill. Accordingly, it lost no time. And ere long, its every member became a proficient in tactics.

When Gen. Wool reviewed the troops at Harper's Ferry, he particularly noticed the Twelfth, and remarked that its manœuvrings could not be surpassed by Regulars.

When the Eighty-Seventh Ohio reached Harper's Ferry, hungry, wet, and weary, Col. Wm. G. Ward, then commandant of the Twelfth, called upon his regiment to send them a large quantity of coffee, boiled and prepared. This may seem an incident unworthy of notice, but any soldier who served in the field will duly appreciate it. And the Ohio Regiment appreciated it too. For immediately thereafter they gratefully acknowledged the exhilarating beverage, in a series of complimentary resolutions.

The Twelfth Regiment's term of service expired on the 27th of August, 1862. But, instead of returning to New York, as did other regiments, it volunteered to remain till the 15th of October, to aid in the defense of the Union works, and in the instruction and formation of regiments sent on under the call for 300,000 three years men.

The Twelfth remained at Harper's Ferry until its communications with the North were cut off by the rebels, who crossed the Potomac after the second battle of Bull Run. Soon after, the rebel army, under Stonewall Jackson, recrossed the Potomac at Williamsport, proceeded to Charlestown, and advanced upon Harper's Ferry, driving in before them Brig. Gen. White's command.

Col. Miles, Commander of Harper's Ferry, made no preparations for its defense, except the cutting down of a few trees on Loudon and Maryland Heights. He sent Col. Ford to Maryland Heights with a large force. But on Friday, September 12th, Col. Ford was repulsed at Solomon's Gap, and compelled to retreat to the place whence he came.

On the morning of September 13, 1862, heavy musketry firing began on Maryland Heights, the enemy attempting to capture that position. Company I of the Twelfth had been drilled in artillery practice; and Capt. Acorn, commanding, took his mountain howitzers to defend the assailed "Heights." In the desperate engagement on Maryland Heights, the One Hundred and

Twenty-Sixth New York became disorganized in consequence of Col. Sherrill being horribly wounded. Col. Ford immediately ordered a retreat, and commanded Capt. Magrath, of the New York Artillery, to spike and destroy his splendid battery of siege guns. At that crisis said order was indeed severe, but obedience, even unto death, is a soldier's duty. Hence the cannon were spiked, dismounted, and hurled down the hill. Capt. Acorn, however, brought his howitzers and ammunition safely down.

After the aforesaid evacuation, the enemy began to show themselves on Maryland Heights. Soon they began to fire on a party of sharp-shooters belonging to the Twelfth. A shell thrown into the midst of the rebels quickly cleared the Heights.

Accounts say that Col. Miles neglected to place Loudon Heights in a proper state of defense. Even his loyalty has been questioned. But it is no more than just that he should be deemed loyal till convicted of disloyalty. No doubt his conduct during the attack on Harper's Ferry was censurable. And to it, the surrender of that stronghold may be attributed.

On Sunday, September 14, 1862, the enemy placed their batteries on and surrounding Loudon Heights. They seemed to be aware that the position which they were about to attack was in a poor state of defense, hence their assault was sudden.

Regardless of the superior numbers and advantageous situation of the foe, the commandant of the Twelfth (Col. Wm. G. Ward) commenced a vigorous shelling of the rebels. So desperate was the attack, and vigorous the defense, that several gunners of the Twelfth sank down at the guns from exhaustion.

Notwithstanding the strenuous efforts of the Northern troops, the secession force got their guns in position, and opened a tremendous fire on the Union camp. Whizzing shots and roaring shells incessantly flew and fell among the ranks of the Twelfth Regiment. Still there was no shrinking from duty nor danger. Both officers and men manifested admirable bravery.

On the following Sunday, the command was ordered to proceed to the front and attack the enemy. Every man in the Regiment seemed electrified at the thought of having a hand-to-hand fight with the foe.

The Regiment formed with the greatest promptness, and forthwith proceeded to Bolivar Heights. On reaching there, the Twelfth found the other regiments in great confusion. But it marched on till it came within musket-shot of a Confederate regiment in ambuscade. They reserved their fire, expecting that the Twelfth had been ordered up to clear them out. Just as the Twelfth was about to charge on the rebels, Col. Miles's Orderly rode up in hot haste, and ordered it to return immediately to Camp Hill. It seems the Regiment had been sent out by mistake, at which Col. Miles manifested great indignation.

On the following evening, however, by permission of Col. Miles, all the cavalry at Harper's Ferry made their escape across the pontoon bridge; but he sternly refused to allow any of the infantry to do likewise.

Orders were given on Sunday evening to throw up earth-works against the next day's attack. The Twelfth worked long and well during the night, and completed a deep trench and a formidable earth-work. At the dawn of the following day, the Twelfth, Col. Wm. G. Ward commanding, resumed the bombardment of Loudon Heights. The officers and men of the Regiment displayed a coolness and an intrepidity that would reflect honor on veterans of a hundred battles. They seemed determined to rout the enemy, and just when victory was within their reach Col. Miles raised the white flag. And thus foiled the grand efforts of loyal troops.

Gen. White then surrendered Harper's Ferry, officers retaining their baggage and swords. The Twelfth, after delivering their arms, faced about, marched back a hundred paces, and bivouacked in sight of their stacked arms. Several of the men, during the night, recovered a large number of muskets at the risk of their lives.

On Monday evening, rolls of the different companies, written on letter paper, were sent to the rebel commander, and the Twelfth discharged as paroled prisoners. During the preceding night, Longstreet's corps crossed the pontoon bridge and joined Stonewall Jackson. The majority of the rebel force marched off on the following morning to Williamsport, where they crossed the Potomac and reinforced Lee at the battle of Antietam.

On Tuesday evening, September 16, 1862, the Twelfth Regiment were ordered to leave the rebel lines. As they marched through Harper's Ferry, the secessionists claimed the colored cooks of the Regiment. Those not claimed were sent to Richmond with all the contrabands at Harper's Ferry.

Immediately thereafter the Regiment returned to New York, where the Mayor and Common Council received them with the honors of the metropolis. Alderman Ottiwell, President of the Reception Committee, and an honorary member of the Regiment, addressed them in most eloquent terms, and cordially thanked them in behalf of the citizens of New York for remaining and doing arduous duty at Harper's Ferry after their term of service had expired. Subsequently, the city authorities gave a sumptuous banquet to the officers of the Regiment.

The following companies and commissioned officers were under command of Col. Ward at Harper's Ferry at the time of its surrender:

Company B, Capt. Hansen, Lieuts. Lynch
and Dauphen . . . . 70 men.
do. C, Capt. Byrne, Lieut. Burns . . 70 do.
do. D, ... 55 do.
do. E, Capt. McAffee . . . . 67 do.
do. F, Capt. Ward, Lieuts. Dyott and
Blair . . . . . . 80 do.
do. H, Capt. Heybourne, Lieut. Glenn . 68 do.
do. I, Capt. Acorn, Lieuts. Ellison and
Millbank . . . . . 73 do.
do. K, Capt. Barclay, Lieut. Higgenbotham . . . . . . 70 do.

Field officers . . . . 3 men.
Staff and non-commissioned staff . . . 7 do.
Co. A, at Fort McHenry, under Capt. Ferry
and Lieuts. Mandeville and Armstrong . . . . 73 do.

Total . . . 636

On the 20th of June, 1863, the command left New York for the third time, to peril their lives in defense of the American Union. Col. Wm. G. Ward was then in command. The regiment arrived at Harrisburg on the 21st, and was quartered in Camp Curtin. Departed thence on the 22d for Marysville, and from that time till the 7th of July, detachments were constantly on duty obstructing roads leading to the camp, felling trees, and digging rifle-pits.

On the last-mentioned date the Regiment moved to Carlisle, arriving there at "midnight's solemn hour," and bivouacking in the public square, while rain fell in torrents. After sleeping that night as weary soldiers sleep, they started at early dawn for Shippensburg, fourteen miles away. Reaching there at sunset they marched nine miles more, in moonlight, to bivouac at Greenville; and on the 8th of July, 1863, arrived at Rock Mount. They reached Chambersburg on the 11th, and there encamped until the 14th, when the Regiment was ordered to Greencastle.

Just about this time riots broke out in the metropolis. The Government, knowing the excellent discipline of the Twelfth and its superior skill in street firing, ordered it to New York to suppress the rioters. As soon as it reached the city, heavy details were "told off," and ordered to protect the City Hall, guard the Gas Works, and other points of importance.

The Regiment's headquarters were at the City Hall, where some of the companies elected commissioned officers.

Pursuant to orders from Division and Brigade headquarters, this Regiment paraded on Thursday, October 1, 1863, in full fatigue dress, armed and equipped, and took part in the reception of the officers of the Russian Fleet by the city authorities.

Pursuant to a resolution of the Board of Officers, this command paraded, fully armed and equipped, on the 11th of June, 1864, and participated in the reception of the Thirty-Ninth Regiment, N. Y. V., " Garibaldi Guard." On the 12th of the same month it paraded as funeral escort to the remains of Col. Orlando H. Morris, late of the Sixty-Sixth, N. Y. V.

The following extract is from the report of Col. J. H. Liebenau, Inspector General:

"October 12, 1866.—Inspected this Regiment, which, owing to stormy weather, I was obliged to do in their armory. This is one of the regiments of which the Division and the city of New York have just cause to be proud. The discipline of the Regiment is unsurpassed. They are well and handsomely uniformed. The manual of arms, the loadings and firing by file, company, wing, and battalion, were handsomely executed, and reflected great credit on the officers and men, showing that officers who are earnest and untiring in their efforts, are sure to succeed in building and sustaining a good and effective regiment, such as is the Twelfth.

"COL. J. H. LIEBENAU."

HONORARY ROLL.

Col. HENRY G. STEBBINS, First Commandant of the Regiment. Elected September, 1847.

Lieut. Col. JOHN J. ASTOR. Elected September, 1847.

Rev. J. T. DALY, First Chaplain. Appointed September, 1847.

Surgeon A. BURDETT. Appointed September, 1847.

Paymaster F. W. COOLIDGE. Appointed September, 1847.

Engineer J. LIVINGSTON. Appointed September, 1847.

Quartermaster T. C. FIELDS. Appointed September, 1847.

First Adjut. J. B. STEARNS. Appointed September, 1847.

Col. RICHARD FRENCH. Elected June, 1856.

Lieut. Col. HART. Elected June, 1856.

Col. JOHN S. COCKS. Elected April 25, 1857. He is the author of the best military law ever enacted in the Legislature of the Empire State. A system of street firing was invented by him, and incorporated by the Adjutant General in the State Regulations. Col. Cocks resigned on the 16th day of November, 1858.

Lieut. Col. H. A. WEEKS. Elected April 25, 1857; resigned May 30, 1859.

Maj. WILLIAM WATTS. Elected April 25, 1857; resigned November 16, 1858.

Maj. Gen. DANIEL BUTTERFIELD, U. S. A., was elected Commandant of the Twelfth Regiment on the 18th day December, 1860.

On the 15th of April, 1861, he served as First Sergeant of the battalion organized for the defense of Washington. On the 19th of the same month he was ordered to report with his regiment, the Twelfth N. Y. S. M., to the General-in-Chief, of the United States Army, at the national capital. In compliance with said order, he sailed from New York, with his command, on the 21st day of April, 1861; arrived at Fortress Monroe on the 23d, tendered aid to the garrison, but none being required, sailed for Annapolis. In May, 1861, he led with the Twelfth, the first movement across the Long Bridge into Virginia, under Gens. Mansfield and Heintzelman.

On the 6th of July, 1861, he was ordered with the Twelfth, to Gen. Patterson's column, at Martinsburg, Va., and shortly after having reported there, a brigade was placed under his command. Said brigade consisting of four New York regiments, and among them the Twelfth. He moved with Patterson's column until July 21, 1861. Then, he was intrusted with the defenses of Bolivar Heights, till the 3d of August, the date of the evacuation of Harper's Ferry, just two weeks beyond the Regiment's term of service.

On the 5th of August, 1861, he was mustered out of service in New York, as Colonel of the Twelfth Regiment. He received, on this occasion, a complimentary order from Gen. Banks. While acting as Colonel of the Twelfth N. Y. S. M., he was appointed Lieutenant Colonel of the Twelfth United States Infantry, Regular Army. Rank to date from May 14, 1861.

On the 7th of September, 1861, Gen. Butterfield was appointed Brigadier General of Volunteers, and assigned to the command of the Third Brigade, Porter's Division (the famous Light Brigade). He led his "Light Brigade" at the dreadful siege of Yorktown; through the desperate battles of Hanover Court House, Mechanicsville,

Gaines's Mills, Turkey Bend, and Malvern Hill. Though dangerously wounded at the latter engagement, he remained on duty, like one determined to become a martyr for his country.

He commanded the detachments sent to the south side of the James River, to cover the withdrawal of McClellan's forces. At Groveton, or second Bull Run, he commanded the First Division of the Fifth Army Corps.

On the 16th of November, 1862, he assumed command of the Fifth Army Corps, and fought in the hard-fought fight of Fredericksburg. On the 29th of November, 1862, he was appointed Major General of Volunteers. On the 26th of January, 1863, Maj. Gen. Hooker appointed him Chief of Staff of the Army of the Potomac.

About this time, and while performing the aforesaid duties, he originated the system of calls, picket and outpost duty. He devised the present beautiful coat of arms of the Twelfth Regiment, and the Corps Badges and Flags that were adopted and worn by the Grand Army.

Gen. Butterfield participated in the memorable battle of Chancellorsville, and was requested by Gen. Meade, who relieved Gen. Hooker, to remain on duty with him as Chief of Staff. He served accordingly, and gallantly fought in the terrific battle of Gettysburg, where he was so severely wounded, that he was compelled to retire from the field.

On the 22d of August, 1863, he entered on temporary duty with Gen. Hooker, at Washington. In the following October he was ordered, as Chief of Staff, with Gen. Hooker's command, to reinforce Rosecrans' Army of the Cumberland, Gen. Butterfield's position placed him in the thickest of the conflict. He participated in the battles of Wauhatchie, Lookout Mountain, Mission Bridge, Tenn.; Ravine Creek, and Ringgold, Ga. In February, 1864, Gen. Grant ordered him to convey important dispatches to Gen. Sherman, at Meridian, Miss. After his return, in April, 1864, he was assigned to the command of the Third Division. This command he held during the Atlantic campaign, till renewed attacks of the fever contracted during the peninsular campaign of 1862, compelled him again to leave the field. Scarcely had he recuperated, when he was exposed to the brunt of the battles of Buzzard Roost, Reseca, Cassville, Gilgal Church, Dallas, New Hope Church, Culp's Farm, Kenesaw, and Lost Mountain.

On the 1st of July, 1863, while doing duty as Major General of Volunteers, he was promoted to the Colonelcy of the Fifth Infantry, Regular Army. On the 13th of March, 1865, he was appointed Brevet Major General United States Army, for gallant and meritorious conduct on the battle-field. After a series of brilliant achievements, he was, on the 24th of August, 1865, mustered out of the service as Major General of Volunteers, returning to his rank in the Regular Army.

Gen. Butterfield, is now Chief of the General Recruiting Department of the United States, at New York. His headquarters are in the magnificent Army Building, corner of Greene and Houston Streets. His affable and courteous demeanor, his generosity and noble character, have won for him a host of admiring friends.

Major General Francis C. Barlow.

"*Dulce et decorum est, pro patria mori.*" Thus, in the expressive language of the Roman bard, spoke Francis C. Barlow, when traitorous hands fired at the time-honored walls of Fort Sumter. He naturally abhorred slavery and hated rebellion. His friends knew that he was a man who always practiced his theories; but little did they dream that an intellectual young lawyer, with a large business and bright prospects, would enter as a private among the "boys in blue." Mr. Barlow forgot personal danger and comforts, when the destruction of our Republic was threatened.

Unostentatiously he joined the Twelfth Regiment, as a private, in Company F, on the 20th of April, 1861. The purity, sincerity, and nobility of his character, forbid us attributing this remarkable condescension to anything, save patriotism. On the 21st of April, 1861, he departed with his regiment for Washington, to defend the nation's capital.

> "All honor to him who, when danger afar
> Had lighted for ruin his ominous star,
> Left pleasure, and country, and kindred behind,
> And sped to the shock on the wings of the wind."

Unlike the majority of privates, Mr. Barlow, while in camp, assiduously applied himself to the study of military tactics. His time was equally divided between duty, study, and repose. Merit so uncommon, could not remain long unappreciated. Hence, Col. Butterfield, who always rewarded genuine merit, offered him the position of First Lieutenant, in Company F, Twelfth Regiment, which he accepted.

Having fulfilled his period of enlistment, he returned to New York. Whilst internal enemies and external foes, were striving to demolish the gigantic and beautiful proportions of our Commonwealth, he could not remain inactive. Hence, after the organization of the Sixty-First New York, he was appointed its Lieutenant Colonel. His capacious intellect, quickly learned, as if by intuition, company evolutions, grand charges of brigades, and all the terrible and sublime machinations of war.

Soon he was assigned, with his regiment, to the Army of the Potomac, under Gen. McClellan. During the dreary months of Autumn and Winter of 1861, Lieut. Col. Barlow resolutely and carefully studied every chapter, in the books of tactics appointed for the army. His superiors easily perceived, that he was master of the art of war ; hence, he was promoted to the rank of Colonel, when northern legions marched to the siege of Yorktown.

After the lapse of a few fearful days, was fought the terrific battle of Fair Oaks. Never was American valor so severely tested. During the bloody conflict, Col. Barlow's regiment lost its color-bearer and four of the color guard. The brave Gen. Howard, having lost an arm, the command of his brigade devolved on Col. Barlow. At the never-to-be-forgotten battle of Antietam, he proved himself the bravest of the brave. To his eyes, on that occasion, death seemed despoiled of its terrors. He was shockingly wounded in the groin and breast. The most eminent physicians and surgeons, pronounced his wounds curable, only by the Physician at whose command, Lazarus came forth from the tomb. And that Physician, through the instrumentality of a faithful and priceless wife, healed the wounded hero.

Scarcely had he recovered, when treason concentrated its forces at Chancellorsville. Through the long battle there fought, he gallantly led a victorious brigade ; and when leagued rebels poured upon the sunny slopes of Pennsylvania, Gen. Barlow led the same brigade through the brunt of that horrible engagement. Midst the bursting of shells and the thundering of cannon, when "death shots fell thick and fast," he fearlessly rode in front of his line, encouraging the troops and exhorting them to remain steadfast.

"The slayer death is everywhere, and many a form hath he."

Four bullets struck Gen. Barlow, and he fell from his horse to the ground. Still the fierce fight raged, and the prostrate, bleeding General, lay on the field, exposed to the fire of friend and foe. Whilst in that deplorable condition, "he found not a generous friend, nor a pitying foe," till night's sable mantle fell upon the gory ground. When the mild moon rose up slowly and looked calmly down on the corpse-strewn battle-field, he was found by the rebel General, Early, who, while passing, discovered his rank. Supposing the spark of life to have fled, Gen. Early, though a traitor, yet a man, paused with his staff officers to learn his name, muttering in grum accents : " We can do nothing for that dead general save to give him a decent burial." Though his life-blood was fast flowing away, Gen. Barlow raised his bleeding head and feeble voice, and gave Early this grave reply : " I will live to fight you yet, General." As if gifted with knowledge of the future, these words, were fully verified, at the battle of Spottsylvania Court House.

In 1864, Gen. Barlow resumed his command, and participated in the great battles of the Wilderness. During one of these conflicts he captured a whole division of Gen. Early's troops, commanded by Gen. Johnson, with forty pieces of artillery and other valuable spoils. He was promoted to a Major Generalship, while the army lay in front of Petersburg ; and when rebellion fought its last fight before Richmond, he had the gratification of beholding, the great stubborn army of the South conquered, by the valiant troops of the North.

Gen. Barlow was nominated by the Union party, of the State of New York, in the Autumn of 1865, for the office of Secretary of State. The Democrats nominated Gen. Slocum, as an opposition candidate ; but Gen.

Barlow was elected, by a majority of 28,000. His excellent executive abilities, rendered him an honor to the Government of the Empire State.

The Twelfth Regiment is proud, to have his noble name and heroic deeds, on its honorary roll. Not without cause ; for, what other regiment in our vast Republic, can name a graduate from its ranks, with a character so *illustrious* and *brave*, as that of Maj. Gen. Francis C. Barlow ?

He now fills the important position of United States Marshal, for the Southern District of New York.

Brig. Gen. William G. Ward.

This gentleman is a graduate of Columbia College, of the city of New York. He enlisted in the Twelfth Regiment on the 4th of March, 1854, as a private, in Company F. He served in all the non-commissioned grades, and was elected Captain of said company. On the 22d of January, 1857, Col. Cocks appointed him Adjutant of the Twelfth Regiment. In the month of March, 1860, he raised two new companies, which necessarily involved no small expenditure of personal wealth. Narrow-minded parties, jealous of his popularity, preferred charges against him that caused his arrest, but, when tried by a court-martial, he was honorably discharged.

On the 25th of May, 1860, he was unanimously elected Major of the Twelfth Regiment, and filled said position till the 25th of the following November, when he was chosen Lieutenant Colonel of the aforesaid command. He went to the seat of war with his regiment (Col. Butterfield commanding) in 1861.

On the 25th of October, 1861, he was elected Commandant of the Twelfth, vice Col. Butterfield promoted. He led his regiment to the seat of war in 1862, and manifested firmness, self-denial, and bravery at the battle of Harper's Ferry. He gave to his men a noble example of heroism and valor ; and he sympathized with them. Frequently during the siege did he relieve, in person, the exhausted gunners. His presence dispelled fear, however great the danger.

During the campaign of 1862, he acted for a time as Brigadier General.

In 1863 he went with his regiment, on what was termed the Pennsylvania campaign. The previous service of the Twelfth had worn out its uniforms and equipments. To obtain funds from the State or National

Treasuries, to purchase new uniforms, was a slow and an uncertain process. Hence, Col. Ward, with rare, but characteristic munificence, defrayed the greater part of the expense incurred in uniforming and equipping the Twelfth for the Pennsylvania campaign. It is stated, that ten thousand dollars would not cover the amounts which he has advanced from his private fortune, for the maintenance of the Twelfth Regiment, since the date of his first commission in the same.

In the month of November, 1866, Col. Ward was unanimously elected Brigadier General of the First Brigade, N. G. S. N. Y. This position he now fills, with honor to himself and entire satisfaction to all parties interested in or connected with the regiments which constitute his brigade.

BREVET BRIG. GEN. FRED. T. LOCKE.

This gentleman's military connection with the Twelfth Regiment comprises a period of more than thirteen years. He was a member of Company G, "Independence Guard," from which the Regiment subsequently took its distinctive name. He passed through the various non-commissioned grades, and was promoted from the post of First Sergeant, to the office of First Lieutenant. The year previous to the rebellion he was made Adjutant of the Twelfth, under Col. Butterfield. In this capacity he served the Regiment during the first three months' campaign of the war. Immediately after he was appointed, by the President, to the important position of Assistant Adjutant General of Volunteers. He was assigned to Porter's Division, Army of the Potomac. In this capacity he acted until the capture of Yorktown. After the formation of the Fifth Army Corps, in May, 1862, he was made its Adjutant General, and promoted to a Lieutenant Colonelcy. He continued in this position during the continuance of the war. In nearly all the engagements by the Potomac Army, he fought. In the campaign under Gen. Pope he also manifested incomparable bravery. On the 8th of May, 1864, Brevet Brig. Gen. Locke, whilst gallantly fighting under Gen. Grant, was dangerously wounded at the battle of Spottsylvania Court House. The wounds received there, were so severe, that he was necessitated to remain inactive for five weary weeks. But at the end of that time he rejoined his command, though not entirely healed.

In the Autumn of 1864, he was promoted to a full Colonelcy, for distinguished gallantry, and meritorious service in the battles and marches of the campaign.

On the 9th day of April, 1865, that eventful day, whose name and date are synonymous with the overthrow of treason, Gen. Locke had the satisfaction of witnessing the surrender of Lee and his defeated army. A few weeks afterward, he was appointed Brevet Brigadier General, for faithful service and conspicuous gallantry, at the battle of Five Forks.

Among the many heroes of the late war, it is difficult to find one whose record is more brave and brilliant than Gen. Locke's.

The following list of battles, in which he participated, eulogizes him more than any language which could be used in these pages. His name is identified with the severest engagements of the war, for the suppression of the rebellion.

He commanded at the siege of Yorktown, at the battles of Hanover Court House, Mechanicsville, Gaines's Mills, Turkey Bend, Malvern Hill, second Bull Run, Antietam, Fredericksburg, Chancellorsville, Gettysburg, Wilderness, Spottsylvania Court House, Appomatox Court House, and Five Forks.

His term of service comprised a period of four years and five months. During three years of said period, he performed the arduous and responsible duties of Adjutant General and Chief of Staff, of the largest corps in the army.

It has been the good fortune of Gen. Locke to receive the most flattering and complimentary testimonials from Gens. Butterfield, Barry, Chamberlain, and Grant.

Col. John Ward.

This gentleman is a brother of Brig. Gen. Ward. Like the latter, he is in figure dignified, in manner affable and courteous, or *suaviter in modo, sed fortiter in re*. He graduated at Columbia College in 1858, at the Columbia Law School in 1860, and at the University Medical College in 1864. His knowledge of military tactics is thorough.

In the year 1861 Col. Ward joined the Twelfth Regiment, as First Lieutenant of Company A. In the latter part of June, 1861, he was unanimously elected Captain of said company, but resigned the position in February, 1862.

In March, 1862, he again entered the Twelfth, being chosen Captain of Company F.

On Friday, July 26, 1861, Col. Ward, then Captain of Company A, led one of four companies commanded by Capt. Huson, crossed the Shenandoah, and occupied the celebrated block-houses built on Loudon Heights by the rebels under Gen. Joseph Johnston. The command held the block-houses till after the evacuation of Harper's Ferry by Gen. Banks. In 1862 Col. Ward went a second time to the seat of war, with the Twelfth Regiment. During this campaign he commanded Company F. His daring and fearless spirit, his remarkable power of expelling fear and instilling courage, were notorious throughout the Regiment. Hence he was chosen, at a time when the bravest dreaded to go outside the lines, to reconnoitre Loudon Heights. He scouted for miles through the country surrounding said heights; and this he did at the peril of his life.

When the siege of Harper's Ferry began, Col. (then Capt.) Ward crossed the pontoon bridge, with Surgeon Draper, to reconnoitre. Immediately thereafter rebel sharpshooters appeared on Maryland Heights, and opened a *sharp fire* on the party.

On his return from Harper's Ferry, he commanded Company F, until October, 1865, when he was elected Major of the Twelfth. On the promotion of Col. Wm. G. Ward to the command of the First Brigade, Major John Ward was elected Colonel, on the 4th of January, 1867.

If all our regiments were commanded by gentlemen of intelligence, wealth, and Christian character, like Col. John Ward, the National Guard would be, what legislators meant it should be, the defense and glory of the Empire State.

Rev. Stephen H. Tyng, Jr.

This eminent divine received his commission as Chaplain of the Twelfth Regiment, on the 18th day of June, 1863. He accompanied it during the Pennsylvania campaign, and like St. Paul, made himself "all things to all men," for the Gospel's sake. Hence his success in performing the important and sacred duties of his office. In camp as in city, he manifested the genuine spirit of a noble minister of the Lord.

The suavity of manners, geniality, unpretentious bearing, ardent zeal and exalted intelligence of Rev. Stephen H. Tyng, jr., have given him a wonderful control over the minds, not only of the officers and members of the Twelfth Regiment, but also of all who have had the happiness to hear his voice or feel his influence. He is a prime mover in every enterprise inaugurated to spread the Gospel, or alleviate the woes of the poor and abandoned in this great metropolis.

> "Oh, blessed Charity! Religion mild!
> Thy gentle smiles are never meant to wound;
> No jest hast thou for error's helpless child,
> But holy tears, and love without a bound.
> Thy constant votaries!—they are seldom found."

To attempt a culogy of Rev. S. H. Tyng, jr., a gentleman whose character is so favorably known to the world, would be superfluous. He needs no praise in these pages. Ministers of every denomination love and admire him; and the Twelfth Regiment sincerely hopes that he may continue to be its beloved Chaplain for many years to come.

Lieut. Col. Livingston Satterlee.

This gentleman is a graduate of Brown University. His military career began by raising, a company, called "Brown University Guards." It was composed of 160 young gentlemen, all of whom became distinguished officers in the Union Army during the rebellion. He subsequently received an appointment on the Staff of Gov. Sprague. In 1858 he joined the First Company of the Seventh Regiment, N. G. S. N. Y. After a brief service therein, he was called to serve on the Staff of Gen. (then Col.) Butterfield, as Paymaster of the Twelfth. When the Twelfth Regiment went to the seat of war, in 1861, Lieut. Col. Satterlee was authorized to raise a new company to fill the letter K. In two days he recruited 102 men, whom he conducted to Rocho's Mills, at that time the most exposed and of dangerous position in the Union Army. He was one the few who went to the seat of war immediately after marriage. As soon as he had joined his regiment, it was made known to him that the commissioned officers were not supplied with revolvers. He instantly ordered, on his own account, two thousand eight hundred dollars worth of revolvers, to be presented to the officers of the Twelfth Regiment. During a portion of his term, in 1861, he acted as an officer in the Secret Service. In 1862 he went to the seat of war, as Lieutenant Colonel of the Twelfth Regiment, and commanded for a time at Harper's Ferry. There he also acted as President of the Court-Martial convened to try capital offenses.

Lieut. Col. Satterlee's generous and self-sacrificing disposition is well and favorably known. Whilst many officers carelessly rode by their sick and wearied men, he frequently descended from his saddle and allowed the lame of his command to ride on horseback. When the regiment reached Frederick, Md., none had quarters save the officers, but he nobly refused to accept any other accommodation than those enjoyed by the rank and file.

He is authorized by the Governor of the State of New York to raise a brigade on Staten Island. As soon as it will be organized, he is to be its General. He is of commanding stature and dignified presence; possesses a vigorous, liberal mind, and a memory remarkably retentive. He has a keen sense of the ludicrous and a brilliant wit, which, in addition to an inexhaustible store of pleasant reminiscences, make him an agreeable companion. He has, too, that frank, openhearted generosity and noble unselfishness which render him at once the popular commander and beloved fellow-officer.

Maj. Knox.

Few can boast of a more honorable record than Maj. Knox during his connection with the Twelfth Regiment and during the war. He was a private in the Engineer Corps of this command, and by meritorious conduct was promoted to the rank of Major in the United States Cavalry.

Quartermaster H. T. Arnold,

Appointed April, 1861, acted with the Twelfth during the campaigns of 1861, 1862, and 1863.

Engineer Benjamin S. Church.

This officer, a member of the Twelfth, will be remembered and respected as long as history narrates the battles of Arlington Heights.

Capt. Church was sent forth to reconnoitre in various sections of Virginia. He prepared a map of the country which he traversed during his *reconnoissances;* said map was for the War Department. It was pronounced and proved to be the most accurate map ever presented to the Government. Subsequently he was detached on special duty, with Lieut. Snyder, of the United States Engineers, and chose the sites of the formidable fortifications on Arlington Heights. During the survey he had several narrow escapes from death, being constantly under fire. He was also captured, but, through his dexterity and bravery, escaped from the rebels. Subsequently he was promoted Brigade Major of the Second Brigade.

ENGINEER MERIAN.

This brave young officer was a member of Church's Engineer Corps, in the Twelfth Regiment. On account of meritorious conduct, he was transferred to the Regular Service, and participated in the attack on Charleston, on board the iron-clad Weehawken.

SURGEON THURSTON.

This eminent surgeon was for a long time connected with the Twelfth. His exalted abilities having been communicated to the Surgeon General, he was appointed Chief of the Medical Staff in the West.

ASSISTANT SURGEON WEIR.

This gentleman, on account of his surgical skill, was placed in charge of the General Hospital at Frederick, Md.

PRESENT FIELD AND STAFF OFFICERS OF THE TWELFTH REGIMENT.

Date of Commission.

Colonel, John Ward........................Jan. 24, 1867.
Lieutenant Colonel, Knox McAffee..........Apr. 24, "
Major, Andrus B. Howe....................   "   "
Adjutant, Wm. H. Murphy.................June 6,   "
Engineer, Wm. H. Hays ....Mar. 12,   "
Chaplain, Stephen H. Tyng, jr.............   "   "
Quartermaster, G. L. Maxwell.............Sept. 24, 1866.
Surgeon, Robert D. Nesmith...............July 25, 1868.
Assistant Surgeon, A. R. Merrill..........Oct. 7,   "
Commissary, R. A. Riker..................July 25, "

Non-Commissioned Staff.

Date of Warrant.

Sergeant Major, Wm. H. Kirby ....Nov. 12, 1867.
Quartermaster Sergeant, G. P. Browne....June 26, 1868.
Ordnance Sergeant, Philip Pinkle..........Apr. 21, "
Commissary Sergeant, Wm. F. Raywood....June 11, 1867.
Color Sergeant, Colin Gourley............Feb. 12, "
"   Wm. B. Bliss..............Nov. 18, "
"   Thomas Wilson...........   — 1868.
Hospital Steward, S. G. Spackman........May 10, 1867.
Drum Major, G. L. Strube................   —
Band Master, John G. Otto...............Apr. 27, 1864.

A Company, Twelfth Regiment.

Previous to the joining of this corps with the Twelfth Regiment, in 1847, little is known of its history, except that it was an independent organization, composed of respectable citizens. When, in 1847, it joined this Regiment, it was styled the "Light Guard," and commanded by Capt. Vincent.

This company rendered valuable services to the Union cause during the great struggle between loyalty and treason. It went to the seat of war, in 1861, with the following officers:

Captain, Geo. H. Barr. Subsequently under Capt. John Ward, jr.
First Lieutenant, J. M. Ferry.
Second Lieutenant, W. H. Hoagland.
Second Second Lieutenant, J. M. Mandeville.

Corporal Abner E. Benedict, of this company, was appointed Second Lieutenant, U. S. A., in 1861; distinguished himself in several engagements, and was promoted Captain in the Regular Army. He died while in service at one of the forts in New York Harbor, from his wounds and fever contracted on the field.

Corporal Sealy, of this company, also, rose to the rank of Assistant Adjutant General, and was posted at Hilton Head, South Carolina.

Frederick Thompson, after leaving this corps, became an Aid-de-Camp on Gen. Hooker's Staff, fought in several severe battles, was dangerously wounded, and compelled to leave the field.

S. L. Prankard, after Company A returned from the seat of war, in 1862, went to St. Louis, raised a company of 100 men, distinguished himself in the engagements with the rebel Gen. Price and the Union forces. For gallantry shown at the battle of Fredericktown, he was promoted to the position of Lieutenant

Colonel, and commanded for some time the post of Rolla.

George B. Swan left the company in 1863, removed to Dubuque, Iowa, joined an Iowa regiment, went to Tennessee, and after having been appointed a Major, was killed while reconnoitring inside the enemy's lines.

John McIlvain, after the company's first campaign, went to Wheeling, Va., and became First Lieutenant of the "Union Guard," a company raised through his exertions.

Charles M. Livingston, as soon as the company was mustered out of service, received the appointment of Quartermaster under Gen. Martindale.

Joseph D. Merritt served with the company during the campaigns of 1861, 1862, and 1863, and afterward joined a Connecticut regiment, as Second Lieutenant, but after the battle of Gettysburg was promoted to the office of Lieutenant Colonel.

Capt. J. M. Ferry commanded this company during its stay at Fort McHenry, Baltimore. The qualities which he manifested were an ardent love of discipline, bravery, and self-possession. His Lieutenants at the aforesaid fort were J. M. Mandeville and Armstrong. They were gentlemen fully competent to fulfill the duties of their office.

Thomas Stanton left New York after the Twelfth's return in 1862, joined a Maryland regiment just before the battle of Gettysburg, became a First Lieutenant, and distinguished himself in the last-named engagement.

Hiram McFarlain went with the Regiment through the campaigns of 1861, 1862, and 1863, left New York with the Eighty-Fourth Ohio, fought in ten battles, and came home with the rank of Major.

Joseph Williams, U. S. V., 1861.
Donald McKay, U. S. N., 1861.
Chas. J. Quinn, Irish Brigade, 1861.

Major A. B. Howe, of the Twelfth, was a member of Company A.

Lieut. Wm. H. Hoagland, in N. Y. V., Twelfth Regiment, killed at Fredericksburg.

William H. Murphy, the present Adjutant of the Regiment, enlisted in Company A on the 19th of April, 1861, served during the campaign of that year, and also with his company at Fort McHenry in 1862 (this company being detached for artillery duty at the Fort, whilst the remaining companies of the Regiment were ordered to Harper's Ferry). While in Fort McHenry, he was detailed as First Sergeant of Company A, and remained in that position until the return of the Regiment to New York. While on duty during the riots of 1863, Serg. Murphy was detailed as acting Sergeant Major, and was warranted as such by Col. Wm. G. Ward, September 30, 1863, remaining Sergeant Major for four years. He was appointed Adjutant May 20, 1867, and performs the arduous duties of his office to his own credit and the satisfaction of his superiors.

PRESENT MEMBERS OF A COMPANY.
COMMISSIONED OFFICERS.
                                              Date of Commission.
Captain, B. D. Bacon (resigned 1869)......June 8, 1867.
  First Lieutenant J. E. Dowley, of Company I, detailed to command this corps.
First Lieutenant, G. S. Burger (resigned)   Mar. 8, "
Second Lieutenant, J. H. Horsfall.......... — 1869.

NON-COMMISSIONED OFFICERS.
SERGEANTS.
                                              Date of Warrant.
First Sergeant, Wm. Irvine...............Nov. 15, 1865.
Second Sergeant, John Jackson...........Jan. 4, 1864.
Third Sergeant, George W. Mitchell.......Nov. 15, 1865.
Fourth Sergeant, Theo. Hoffstetter........Dec. 2, 1867.
Fifth Sergeant............................

DRUMMER.
Peter Brown........................Nov. 25, 1867.

CORPORALS COMPANY A.
H. R. F. Koechling....................Aug. 5, 1867.
Francis Losee, jr.....................Dec. 2, "
A. G. Hoffstetter..................... "   "

PRIVATES COMPANY A.
                                              Date of Certificate.
Avery, Wm. H........................Sept. 1, 1862.
Ambault, Wm.........................Oct. 29, 1866.
Andrews, John.......................June 11, 1868.
Babcock, F. C.......................May 11, 1863.
Booth, Solomon......................Feb. 8, 1864.
Brister, J. E.......................Sept. 26, "
Bennett, G. M.......................Oct. 29, 1866.
Birch, Wm. E........................Feb. 10, 1868.
Boessing, Henry.....................June 11, "
Carter, Henry.......................Jan. 22, 1865.
De Merseman, John...................Feb. 29, 1864.
Dowling, James......................July 2, 1866.
Deihl, Henry........................June 1, 1868.
Ettlen, Louis.......................June 11, "

TWELFTH REGIMENT.

Fenssel, George.........................July 23, 1866.
Gladding, Asa W......................Oct. 3, 1864.
Gallagher, Wm. R.....................May 15, 1865.
Goodfellow, James D..................Nov. 5, 1866.
Hendry, Thomas.......................June 11, 1867.
Hood, Wm. H..........................Oct. 26, 1868.
Jones, Isaac R........................Sept. 7, 1863.
Jones, G. W...........................Feb. 1, 1864.
Kinzie, Thomas........................Sept. 1, 1862.
Kocheling, H. R. F....................Nov. 6, 1865.
Lenicke, A. W.........................Feb. 8, 1864.
Lockwood, O. H ....July 23, 1866.
Loup, John............................May 22, 1861.
Luckhardt, Fred.......................Jan. 6, 1868.
Larue, Wm. H.........................April 3, 1865.
Lottenberger, Chas....................June 11, 1868.
Mason, Rodney ....Dec. 1, 1863.
Mitchell, J. E.........................July 16, 1866.
Murphy, J. E..........................Oct. 1,   "
Muth, John............................June 11, 1868.
Myers, Chas...........................   "   "
Nelson, John ....   "   "
Porter, G. G..........................Jan. 25, 1864.
Pettit, A. S...........................Nov. 6, 1865.
Pidgeon, Samuel.......................June 11, 1868.
Rogers, John..........................Nov. 1, 1858.
Reich, F. B...........................June 11, 1868.
Robert, John..........................   "   "
Roemer, Fred..........................Oct. 5,   "
Sinner, John ....Sept. 28,   "
Schanton, Chas. H.....................Oct. 2, 1865.
Smith, Chas. C........................Mar. 31, 1862.
Sexton, John..........................Oct. 1,   "
Werknick, Jacob.......................Oct. 26, 1868.
Wood, Thomas T.......................Feb. 11, 1867.
Welden, Wm. H........................Jan. 25, 1864.

B Company, Twelfth Regiment.

Previous to 1847, this corps was known as the City Musketeers, commanded by Captain Palmer. Several facts relative to the past history of the company are here presented for the gratification of its members. Said facts, or at least some of them, may not be precisely *ad rem*, still, they are given in full, at the request of ex-officers of Company B.

On Thursday, the 14th day of October, 1852, the "Citizens Corps," under the command of Capt. Thomas Kirk, paraded for their second annual excursion, and the pleasure and military ardor aroused on that occasion led to the formation of the Washington Light Guard.

At a meeting of the members of the "Citizens Corps," held at the Bowery Hotel (395 Bowery), on the evening of January 12, 1853, it was resolved to form a military company, to be attached to some regiment of the State Militia, and the company name was decided to be the "Washington Light Guard." At a subsequent meeting officers were elected as follows:

For Captain, Thomas Kirk.
" First Lieutenant, Peter M. Willson.
" Second Lieutenant, John H. Stokes.
" Orderly Sergeant, Charles Russell.
" Secretary, Henry W. Genet. (State Senator.)

Charles Russell shortly after resigned as a member of the company, and as the position of Orderly became vacant, Edwin P. Whitcomb was elected Orderly, and acted as such until his time expired.

A petition, signed by the members, was forwarded to the Governor of the State, requesting that the company might be placed in some infantry regiment doing duty in this city.

The City Musketeers (Company B, Twelfth Regiment) were about disbanding at this time (early in the Summer, 1853), and their charter was duly transmitted to Capt. Kirk and his company. First company parade of the Washington Light Guard took place November 22, 1853.

At the yearly meeting, held January 5, 1854, by resolution, the 22d day of February was adopted as its anniversary. The company at this time was fully admitted to the Twelfth Regiment, and had attended regimental drills.

Capt. Thomas Kirk died April 3, 1854, and was buried on Tuesday, April 4, 1854.

The following companies, in connection with Company B, parading by the order of Col. Stebbins:

Lafayette Fusileers, Capt. French.
Baxter Blues, Capt. Waterbury.
City Blues, Capt. ——

On May 11, 1854, the following officers were elected: Captain, Thomas Thomas (late of the Cambrian Musketeers); Second Lieutenant, Henry W. Genet, now State Senator. At this election Col. Stebbins, Lieut. Col. Hart, and Adjut. Stearns, were present.

First Parade of this company took place on May 31, 1854.

Second Parade, July 4, 1854.

April 25, 1855.—Capt. Thomas died. April 29, 1855—Funeral of Capt. Thomas; the following companies parading with Company B: Cambrian Musketeers, Lieut. Short; National Guard (of Brooklyn, L.I.), Captain Sprague; and Tomkins Blues, Company C; Baxter Blues, Company H; City Blues, Company D; Independence Guard, Company E; Baxter Guard, Company I; Lafayette Fusileers, Company F; and Engineer Corps, all of the Twelfth Regiment; the whole forming a battalion under command of Capt. Besson.

The offices of Captain, First Lieutenant, and Second Lieutenant, being vacant, an election was ordered to fill vacancies, on June 4, 1855, with the following result:

Captain, Benjamin E. Bremner; Second Lieutenant, William Gee; no name being submitted for First Lieutenant.

July 16, 1855.—Resignation of Capt. Bremner accepted.

The resignation of Capt. Bremner left the company under the command of Second Lieut. Gee. An election was ordered by Col. R. French, to take place on the evening of September 24, 1855, and which resulted in the election of John H. Dixon as Captain, and Frederick Frye as First Lieutenant.

On May 19, 1856, William Huson (late Captain of Company A, Tenth Regiment, N. Y. S. M.) was duly elected Captain of this company.

At a special meeting of the company, held on October 31, 1859, it was resolved to apply for a charter for a company of the Twenty-Second Regiment, said regimental district being vacant at the time. A roll was prepared and signed by all the active members of the late Company B, Twelfth Regiment.

An election was held on this evening for Captain, which resulted in the election of Capt. William Huson.

At a meeting of the company held on March 14, 1859, Private Phinny Ayres was elected First Lieutenant; N. L. Hanson, Second Lieutenant; A. K. P. Dennett, Orderly Sergeant.

Lieut. P. Ayres' resignation as First Lieutenant was accepted on December 12, 1859.

February 15, 1860.—Private E. B. Stead was elected First Lieutenant of this company.

From this. until the time the Regiment was ordered to Washington, in April, 1861, nothing of importance occurred as relating peculiarly to this company.

On April 21, 1861, in compliance with General Order No. 12, Twelfth Regiment, the following active members of Company B embarked for Washington:

Captain, William Huson.
Second Lieutenant, N. L. Hanson.
Orderly Sergeant, A. K. P. Dennett.

TWELFTH REGIMENT.   51

Second Sergeant, James C. W. Brenner.
Third   "   John R. Hamilton.
Fourth   "   William A. Shaw.
Fifth   "   Edward Willcocks.
First Corporal, Arnold Goodwin.
Private James H. Ashe.
   "   C. McKinlay.
   "   John R. Niel.
   "   William F. Raywood.
   "   Lewis L. Stewart.
   "   John T. Underhill.
   "   John La Rue.
2 Drummers.
95 Volunteers.

First Lieut. E. B. Stead being unable to leave with the Company on its departure (subsequently went out as Captain of a company in the Second Regiment, N. Y. S. M.), the position of First Lieutenant being vacant, the following promotions were made :

Second Lieut. N. L. Hansen to First Lieutenant.
Ord. Sergt A. K. P. Dennett to Second Lieutenant.
Corporal Arnold Goodwin to Orderly Sergeant.

Subsequently, Ord. Sergt. Arnold Goodwin was promoted to Second Lieutenant by Brevet, and Second Sergt. C. L. W. Brenner was appointed Orderly Sergeant.

Shortly after this, Capt. Wm. Huson resigned, for the purpose of accepting a captaincy in a regiment at that time organizing.

On or about the same time, the largest portion of the members' time having expired, they obtained their discharge, and the organization formed in January 12, 1853, came virtually to an end.

The following officers, non-commissioned officers, and privates of B Company volunteered their services to the Government during the late war.

Wm. Huson, late Captain of B Company, at the return of the Regiment from the three months' campaign, resigned his position as Captain of the Company, and with a number of the old officers of the Twelfth, N. Y. S. M., started the organization of a regiment for the purpose of offering their services to the Government for three years, or during the war. Subsequently, the volunteers raised were consolidated into five companies, with orders to report to the Twelfth Regiment, N. Y. S. V. (from Oneida County), at that time stationed at Upton's Hill, Va. Capt. Huson received a commission from the Governor of this State (E. D. Morgan), bearing date of February 3, 1862, appointing him as Captain of B Company, Twelfth Regiment, N. Y. S. V. He left with his command shortly after, and joined the Twelfth Regiment, N. Y. S. V., at Upton's Hill, Va., participated with the Regiment in the following battles and skirmishes:

Yorktown, April 5, 1862.
Yorktown, April 20, 1862.
Hanover Court House, May 27, 1862.
Gaines's Mill, June 27, 1862.
Turkey Bend, June 30, 1862.
Malvern Hill, July 1, 1862.
Second Bull Run, August 29, 1862.
Second Bull Run, August 30, 1862.
Antietam, September 16, 1862.
Antietam, September 17, 1862.
Shipperstown Ford, September 20, 1862.
Fredericksburg, acted as Field Officer of the day for the brigade in the battle, which lasted during the 15th, 16th, and 17th of December, 1863.
Chancellorsville, 1st, 2nd, and 3d of May, 1863.

At the battle of Chancellorsville, the term of the portion of the members of the Twelfth, from Oneida County, having expired (this being originally one of the two years regiments), the members from New York City were consolidated into four companies, and Capt. Huson ordered to take command; their name was at the same time changed to the "New York Battalion." This battalion was ordered out on a reconnoitre, and becoming lost from the brigade for twenty-four hours, bivouacked for the night on the banks of the Rapidan and Rappahannock, at a place called Scott's Mill, and on the day following rejoined the brigade.

Capt. Huson was mustered out of the service on July 1, 1863, having been rendered supernumerary by the consolidation of the battalion into two companies for Provost Guard duty at the headquarters of the Fifth Army Corps, the companies being placed under command of Capt. H. W. Rider, an old officer of the Twelfth, N. Y. S. M.

Lieut. E. B. Stead joined the Second Regiment, N. Y. S. M., at the commencement of the war, and received a commission as Captain.

Lewis L. Stewart enlisted as private in the Sixty-Sixth Regiment, N. Y. S. V., and rose to the rank of Captain in same regiment.

The following members of this corps rendered valuable services to the Government during the war:

G. G. Tracy became a Colonel of the Eighty-Sixth, Pennsylvania, after the battle of the Wilderness.

J. D. Perry, on account of gallantry shown before Yorktown, received the commission of Major in a Long Island Regiment.

Wm. O'Brien, formerly a Corporal in this Company, became a Captain of Volunteers before the termination of the rebellion.

Thomas Shea fought in sixteen battles, and when dying of his wounds in the Washington Hospital, requested that the name of Company B, Twelfth Regiment, should be painted on the " board of his grave." Company B will yet build him a monument.

J. L. Benjamin, after the Company's last term of service had expired in 1863, removed to Baltimore, and soon after was commissioned as First Lieutenant in Company I, Fifth Maryland Volunteers.

H. C. Byrne, who was a private in this company, in 1862, is now a Captain in the Regular Army, doing duty in New Mexico.

Edward J. Jennings, formerly a corporal in this company, was promoted to the office of Major in the Sixty-Ninth Kentucky Volunteers. While reconnoitring the country around Murfreesboro, he was captured by a party of rebels, and when attempting to escape was unfortunately shot.

Henry C. Plunkett, a relative of the last-named gentleman, was likewise a member of Company B during its, campaigns of 1861, 1862, and 1863. He joined the Eighty-Ninth New York Volunteers, and on account of gallantry shown before Petersburg, was presented with a gold medal and made a line officer in the United States Army.

Jeremiah Sullivan was just of age when this corps first went to the seat of war. He took part in all the regimental campaigns, and subsequently became an aid on the Staff of General Wadsworth.

Isaac Halsey was a private in this Company in 1862. He is now a Captain in the United States Army, stationed at Galveston, Texas.

Capt. G. A. Banta, the present Commandant of Company B, has a noble war record. Did space allow, an account of his services during the rebellion would be given in full. Suffice it to say, that he is a high-toned gentleman and a brave officer.

PRESENT MEMBERS OF B COMPANY.

COMMISSIONED OFFICERS.

Date of Commission.

Captain, George A. Banta..............Feb. 22, 1865.
First Lieutenant, James Theo. Burke...... " "
Second Lieutenant, Richard S. Taylor....... " "

NON-COMMISSIONED OFFICERS.

Date of Warrant.

First Sergeant, Eugene Souleyette..........May 3, 1867.
Second Sergeant, Hugh F. Gallagher.......Sept. 6, "
Third Sergeant, Charles H. Opdyke........ " "
Fourth Sergeant, Rufus N. Waller......... " "
Fifth Sergeant, Charles Heizman..........Jan. 11, "

CORPORALS.

William H. Waller.....................Sept. 1, 1868.
Julius E. Karr.............................. " "
John Edlar................................. " "
James L. Conrey........................ " "

DRUMMERS.

Date of Certificate.

Jeremiah Smith........................June 2, 1865.
George W. Brown.....................Oct. 20, "

PRIVATES.

Date of Certificate.

Anton, Francis........................Nov. 23, 1865.
Ahern, William........................July 30, 1866.
Annette, William T...................Sept. 10, "
Anten, James W.......................Nov. 2, "
Archer, Warren S......................Oct. 7, 1867.
Baird, James..........................April 1, 1861.
Bruen, Richard W......................May 8, 1863.
Beach, William H......................May 22, "
Betts, Curtis ....June 9, 1865.
Bauer, Gustave C.......................Aug. 3, "
Bradley, Hugh........................April 1, 1867

Buttle, Henry.....................Jan. 4, 1867.
Boissord, A. E....................Sept. 8, 1865.
Croniu, David E..................May 27, 1862.
Crane, Horace F..................April 28, 1865.
Conway, Joseph L................Sept. 1, "
Chatterton, Stephen..............Nov. 9, 1866.
Casey, Robert....................May 1, "
Cleverly, William................Aug. 29, 1862.
Deems, Samuel M................April 3, 1865.
Douglas, Hugh...................May 19, "
Deibach, Louis C................Aug. 29, 1866.
Dowers, George W...............Sept. 29, 1865.
Dietz, Alfred A..................June 30, 1866.
Demarest, William...............Sept. 7, "
Dietz, Alfred J..................July 2, "
Ernst, Joseph F.................. " "
Fricz, Joseph....................Nov. 2, "
Foster, George..................Nov. 9, "
Huntress, William B.............Sept. 4, 1863.
Hoey, Joseph J.................. " "
Hampsen, John..................June 3, 1864.
Heintz, Jr., J. J.................May 25, 1866.
Hoffmeister, F. L................July 2, "
Hardcastle, John R..............Sept. 7, "
Koose, Charles A................Mar. 24, 1865.
Kirkman, Fred..................Sept. 1, "
Keene, Charles W...............Oct. 27, "
Lonergan, Michael...............Jan. 15, 1864.
Latson, Mortimer E.............Nov. 10, 1865.
Livingstone, William............Aug. 3, 1866.
Langdon, John.................Oct. 19, 1865.
McKinley, Cornelius............Dec. 12, 1859.
McBennett, Jos. C..............Nov. 11, 1862.
McGerold, Arthur...............May 22, 1863.
McDonald, James...............Jan. 27, "
Mason, Francis.................April 14, 1865.
Mahon, Francis P..............June 30, "
Mans, Frederick...............Aug. 3, 1866.
Marvin, Francis J..............May 27, 1862.
Nolte, August..................Feb. 2, 1866.
Page, Thomas T...............May 27, 1862.
Pastill, Thomas................Feb. 2, 1866.
Piest, John J..................Dec. 21, "
Parker, Sherman B............April 28, 1865.
Rainey, G. M.................Mar. 3, "
Rossie, Gustave...............May 26, "
Sibley, Wm. H................May 27, 1862.

Salter, John J.....................Aug. 28, 1865.
Sedwig, Wenne....................Feb. 26, 1866.
Sampson, John A..................July 2, "
Stevens, Samuel W................Aug. 3, "
Van Buren, Peter..................Oct. 25, "
Wamby, Abraham.................Oct. 19, 1866.
Wood, Warren W..................June 9, " .
Waller, Oscar A...................April 21, 1865.
Yager, Emile......................April 28, "
Yager, Francis....................Nov. 2, 1866.
3*

C COMPANY.

This organization, like every company in the Twelfth, existed previous to 1847 as an independent body. At the time of its joining the Regiment it was known as the "Tompkins Blues," under command of Capt. Besson.

The present Commandant, William V. Byrne, being now the senior officer of the Regiment, and the reorganizer of C Company, deserves first mention. He joined the Twelfth in the year 1853, and acted as Commissary Sergeant on board the steamship Columbia, while transporting the Regiment to the seat of war, in 1861. On the 29th of June, of the same year, Col. Butterfield appointed him Sergeant Major, while in Camp Anderson.

On the 26th of August, 1862, he was ordered, with fifty-eight men, to defend the Shenandoah Valley, against the raids of Stewart's Cavalry. On the 14th of September, 1862, in command of Companies C and K, guarded the pontoon bridge at Harper's Ferry.

While in the field this company was noted for its superior drill and discipline, which, of course, are in a great degree attributable to the efficiency of Capt. William V. Byrne.

At the reorganization of the company, in December, 1861, the following were its officers:

Captain, W. V. Byrne.
First Lieutenant, George C. Geissen.
Second Lieutenant, Leon C. Canter.
First Sergeant, Alexander Atchinson.

During its first term of service, in 1861, it was commanded by:

Captain, William Fowler.
First Lieutenant, Charles Whitlock.

Second Lieutenant, William Monteith.
" Lieutenant, J. M. Scribner.

Genett Dykman and Charles Baxter, who distinguished themselves in the Mexican War and in the war against the Confederacy, were active, and are now Honorary Members of this company.

J. C. Shaw, at one time an active member of this company, is a Captain in the United States Army. He fought at Galveston.

Sydney Cornwell, a private, joined a New Hampshire regiment, and returned with the rank of Lieutenant Colonel.

Henry Maguire, an old member of this corps, rose to the position of First Lieutenant in a Monroe County regiment, and fell before Petersburg—that spot which proved so fatal to New York troops.

Hiram Sanford went with the Twelfth through all its campaigns, re-enlisted in a Brooklyn regiment, and became a Second Lieutenant.

F. L. Sherman, a fine-looking soldier, after the Regiment returned from Harper's Ferry, joined the Sixteenth New Jersey as First Lieutenant, and was seriously wounded at Malvern Hill.

George Kunkel went with the company through the campaigns of 1861-2; joined the Fifth Regiment, and rose to the position of Quartermaster. In 1864 he was sent to Fortress Monroe, to aid in the exchange of prisoners. He fell a victim to yellow fever before Lee's surrender.

Henry Hoffman, a relative of the present Governor of New York, left this company in 1863, enlisted in the Seventy-First N. Y. S. M., and for gallantry and meritorious conduct, was promoted to the office of Lieutenant Colonel in the Forty-Eighth New Jersey Volunteers.

William L. Tracy, also once a private in this corps, joined the last-named regiment and became a First Lieutenant.

PRESENT MEMBERS OF C COMPANY.

COMMISSIONED OFFICERS.

                                          Date of Commission.
Captain, William V. Byrne..............Jan. 14, 1862.
First Lieutenant, George C. Geisson.......April 27, 1866.
Second Lieutenant, Leon A. Canter........April 27, "

DRUMMERS.
                                            Date of Certificate.
Joseph Schlosson........................July 12, 1865.
John Priest.............................April 15, 1867.
Nicholas Riley..........................

SERGEANTS.
                                            Date of Warrant.
First Sergeant, Lewis Dunham............May 13, 1867.
Second Sergeant, Edward F. Miles........ "   "
Third Sergeant, Henry W. Forde..........Sept. 16, "
Fourth Sergeant, Mich. H. Kearney.......Mar. 9, 1868.
Fifth Sergeant,

CORPORALS.
John McVay..............................
Geo. Van Wagner........................July 3, 1863.
Andrew C. Shear........................June 22, 1868.
James Van Wagner....................... "   "

PRIVATES.
                                            Date of Certificate.
Byrne, M. H............................Dec. 6, 1861.
Bassford, Sam'l A......................Aug. 28, 1863.
Brady, Wm. F........................... "   3, 1868.
Clifford, Charles......................June 26, 1865.
Clark, George.......................... " 22, 1868.
Demarest, Wm. A........................May 26, 1865.
Desmond, Humphrey...................... " 13, 1867.
Elder, Francis.........................Aug. 2, 1865.
Gorman, Sam'l D........................Nov. 8, 1862.
Gormley, James H.......................June 30, 1865.
Gethings, James B...................... " 25, 1868.
Howard, William........................July 8, "

Hodnet, John..........................Oct. 5, 1866.
Hart, Thomas.........................June 4, "
Howe, Baxter.........................." 2, 1862.
Kuntz, John..........................Sept. 25, "
Lane, John A.........................Oct. 26, 1868.
Lawrence, H. C........................ " "
Muller, George........................June 16, 1866.
Milligan, S. C........................May 19, 1865.
Morgan, Charles A.....................Dec. 12, 1864.
Phelps, James H......................Oct. 5, 1865.
Roshore, John T. B....................Sept. 26, 1864.
Rogers, Wm. F.........................Nov. 13, 1865.
Spackman, S. G. (promoted sergeant).......May 10, 1867.
Schwartz, Frederick....................Oct. 2, 1865.
Stihle, Charles.......................Mar. 5, 1866.
Schneider, Jacob......................July 16, "
Seward, James H......................June 16, 1867.
Sivells, Thomas........................
Shear, Andrew C......................May 19, 1865.
Vanderbeek, John J....................April 1, 1864.
Westervelt, George....................May 26, 1865.
Williams, G. H.......................June 11, 1866.
White, Matthew......................Dec. 2, 1867.

D COMPANY.

Before the formation of the Twelfth Regiment this corps was known as the "City Blues," commanded by Capt. Johnson. Like the other companies, it still retains its distinctive title, in addition to its alphabetical designation.

During its first term of service, it had the following efficient commissioned officers:

Captain, D. Ottiwell.
First Lieutenant, M. Laughran.
Second Lieutenant, Thomas Murray.

J. G. Simpson, formerly a member of this organization, is a line officer of the Regular Army, at present in California.

Henry Reynolds received the appointment of Aide-de-Camp on Gen. Curtis's Staff in Missouri.

John L. Knapp, a private, became a Quartermaster under Gen. Banks.

P. G. Montgomery, for gallantry at Petersburg, was made First Lieutenant under Gen. Butler.

R. M. Jones, for meritorious conduct, was raised from the ranks, whilst on duty before Yorktown, and made a Sergeant Major in a Massachusetts regiment.

Lorenzo Kelly, a private, became First Lieutenant in the Twelfth Ohio.

S. P. Cameron, also a private of this company, was commissioned as Colonel of a colored regiment, and fell at the battle of Fort Pillow.

Richard Jones, now an officer in the Seventh Regiment, N. G. S. N. Y., served seven years in this company, and was honorably discharged.

Capt. H. B. Smith, present Commandant of Company D, has a splendid war record. He participated in several severe engagements during the rebellion. As a tactician, he is not surpassed by any officer in the National Guard. A lengthy account of his exploits would be given were it not that he dislikes notoriety.

PRESENT MEMBERS OF D COMPANY.

COMMISSIONED OFFICERS.
Date of Commission.
Captain, Henry B. Smith..............May 30, 1867.
First Lieutenant, Charles H. Frost........Oct. 4, 1866.
Second Lieutenant, Edward Wood.........   "   "

DRUMMERS.
Date of Certificate.
J. P. Kanaly.........................June 19, 1863.
Wm. Lewis...........................Nov. 2, 1865.
Wm. H. Francis......................Jan. 3, 1867.

SERGEANTS.
Date of Warrant.
First Sergeant, J. H. Wood.............Oct. 23, 1865.
Second Sergeant, Peter B. Wilson........June 17, 1863.
Third Sergeant, Wm. V. Shaw............Sept. 20, 1866.
Fourth Sergeant, Achilles Wood..........Mar. 12, "
Fifth Sergeant, ——— ———. ....

CORPORALS.
Peter Callaghan......................Jan. 2, 1868.
Moses J. Lewin...................... "   "
Andrew Beattie......................Mar. 12, 1866.
Chas. H. Reed.......................Oct. 1, 1868.

PRIVATES.
Date of Certificate.
Appel, Solomon......................Aug. 6, 1868.
Burns, John.........................Mar. 24, 1864.
Beatty, John........................Oct. 25, 1865.
Brown, Henry W....................Dec. 28, "
Bauer, John........................ "   6, 1866.
Cosgrove, John.....................July 3, 1868.
Christman, Philip..................Aug. 29, 1867.
Carroll, Thomas....................Mar. 10, 1865.
Doblen, Marcus....................May 7, 1868.
Erbe, John P.......................July 16, "
Farrell, Michael...................Sept. 17, 1868.
Gilbertson, John...................Dec. 6, 1866.
Hohenstein, John..................June 7, "

Hedler, Gustavus A.....................Aug. 5, 1866.
Keenan, Frank II......................June 14, "
Kavanagh, Garrett.....................Sept. 10, 1868.
Kidney, William.......................May 21, "
Levi, August..........................July 11, 1867.
McMahon, Owen.........................Oct. 9, 1859.
Murphy, J. W..........................Feb. 7, 1860.
Mitchell, Robt........................July 3, "
McMahon, Wm...........................May 14, 1868.
Michael, F............................Sept. 17, 1868.
McDonald, Edward F....................Aug. 20, "
McMahon, James........................June 18, "
Mara, L. P............................May 6, 1862.
Moran, Lawrence....................... " 2, 1867.
Ohmen, Henry..........................June 7, 1866.
Porter, Robert........................May 4, 1865.
Paris, John J.........................Oct. 25, "
Quinlan, Morris.......................April 13, 1864.
Robarts, John.........................Nov. 8, 1866.
Ritter, Philip........................Aug. 5, 1866.
Romain, John..........................Oct. 2, 1862.
Schmohl, Wm. II.......................May 4, 1865.
Sefter, Henry.........................Aug. 29, 1867.
Smith, Wm. J.......................... " "
Sproul, Arthur........................June 8, 1867.
Wier, Patrick.........................Jan. 3, 1867.
Ward, John J..........................May 2, "
Whithock, Henry ....Sept. 12, "
Williamson, James.....................Apr. 13, 1864.

E COMPANY.

Originally this Company was distinguished as "Guard Lafayette," under command of Capt. Leclerc. In addition to its alphabetic title, it is now known as the "Webster Guard."

Brig. Gen. John E. Bendix was the organizer and first Captain of E Company. Its origin dates back to November, 1847. He commanded it for several years after its joining the Twelfth.

The following abbreviated facts relative to him, will no doubt be read with pleasure by those who have known him:

He was promoted Lieutenant Colonel Eleventh Regiment, N. G., August 25, 1858. Organized the Seventh Regiment Volunteers, and elected Colonel April, 1861. Mustered into the United States service April 23, 1861. Embarked for Fortress Monroe, Va., May 26th, arrived at Fortress Monroe May 28th. May 29th, joined expedition under command of Col. Phelps, and took possession of Newport News, Va., May 30th.

June 9th, ordered to take command of detachments of the First Vermont, Fourth Massachusetts Militia, and Seventh N. Y. V., about 900 men, and joined expedition from Fortress Monroe against Big Bethel. Loss to the Seventh, seven killed and twenty wounded.

Resigned position on the 7th, and put in command of the Tenth Regiment N. Y. V. by Gov. Morgan. September 2, 1861, on duty in Fortress Monroe all Winter. April 9 and 10, 1862, commanded guns in the fort during the engagement with the rebel ram Merrimac.

May 9, 1862, joined expedition to Norfolk, Va. May 10, 1862, captured Norfolk, when the flag of the Tenth Regiment was hoisted on Norfolk Custom House, being the first Union flag raised since Virginia seceded.

Commenced fortifications in Norfolk Harbor until June 6, 1862, when he was ordered with his command to report to Gen. McClellan, in front of Richmond.

Joined the Fourth Brigade, Third Division (Regulars), Fifth Corps, June 9, 1862. Engaged in the seven days' fight. Loss in killed and wounded, thirty men. Here Gen. Bendix was slightly wounded in the ankle, but did not leave the field.

Engaged in second Bull Run. Loss, killed and wounded, 160 men, three officers.

Engaged in battle of Antietam. Loss, twenty men. Engaged in battle of Fredericksburg December 12, 1862. Loss in killed and wounded, 160 men, seven officers. Gen. Bendix was wounded in the neck, and forced to leave the field. Sent home on leave of absence for twenty days, on December 25, 1862.

Joined his regiment January 16, 1863. Took command of the Fourth Brigade, Third Division, Second Corps, and remained in command till April 26th, when ordered home to be mustered out of service, the term of his regiment having expired. Mustered out May 7, 1863. Breveted Brigadier General of Volunteers by the President August 28, 1865.

Breveted Brigadier General N. G. September 6, 1866. Organized Third Regiment Infantry (Bendix Zouaves) November 27, 1865, and is now in command of said Regiment.

Gen. Bendix has served in the State N. G. in every grade since 1840. Has been in commission over twenty years, and is the oldest commissioned officer in commission at the present date.

It has been the fortune of this corps to be always commanded by well-qualified officers. In the campaigns of 1861, it was under the following intelligent and active officers :

  Captain, H. W. Ryder.
  First Lieutenant, I. H. Ackerman.
  Second Lieutenant, J. A. Lewis, jr.
  Second Lieutenant, James Gray.

LIEUT. COL. KNOX MCAFFEE.

Among the distinguished ex-members of E Company, Knox McAffee is foremost. He joined the Twelfth on the 29th of April, 1862 ; served as Captain of this company during the campaigns of 1862 and 1863. The Empire State sent not to the seat of war a braver officer than Capt. Knox McAffee. He was promoted to the position of Major on the 4th of January, 1867, and on the 12th of April of the same year elected Lieutenant Colonel of the Twelfth Regiment. As a military instructor he has few equals. His movements are quick and graceful, his voice clear and powerful. When he commands, every man in the battalion distinctly hears. His superior talents, both as a gentleman and an officer, have procured for him the respect and admiration of the officers and members of the Regiment.

Francis Cram, an excellent mathematician, after his discharge from the corps, removed to Annapolis, Md. ; is now an instructor in the Naval Academy.

John J. Dawson was transferred from this Company in 1862. He acted as Commissary at City Point during the stay of the Union Army at that place.

E. M. L. Ehlers joined E Company, Twelfth Regiment, on the 19th of April, 1861. He served with the Twelfth during the campaigns of 1861. On the 12th of September, in the year last mentioned, he was commissioned as Second Lieutenant in the Fifty-Second N. Y. V. For signal bravery, he was promoted as First Lieutenant on the 10th of March, 1862, and was made Captain in the next December. The following battles in which he fought bear ample testimony to his dash and gallantry :

He took part in the battles of Fair Oaks, Gaines's Mill, Peach Orchard, Savage Station, White Oak Bridge, Malvern Hill, Second Bull Run, South Mountain, Antietam, and Fredericksburg. At the last named battle, whilst leading his company through the thick of the fight, he was dangerously wounded by gun-shot through the right lung, arm, and leg. In the bloody battle of Fredericksburg he was severely wounded in the abdomen and side by fragments of a shell. These injuries incapacitated him for active service. Hence he was transferred to the Veteran Reserve Corps on the 10th of December, 1863, with the rank of Captain. For gallant and meritorious services he was Breveted Major, Lieutenant Colonel, and Colonel U. S. V. on the 18th of March, 1865. Since the close of the war he has occupied important positions in the army, lately in Georgia.

One of the remarkable incidents in the history of this company, is the competitive drill which took place between it and the Montgomery Guard, of Boston, *i. e.*, Company I, Ninth Regiment, Massachusetts Militia.

Said drill "came off" on the 30th of July, 1868, at Tompkins Square, in the city of New York. More than twenty thousand people assembled to witness the same. A champion flag was the prize to be awarded the victors. Rules and regulations agreeable to both companies were adopted. Still, so great was the partisan spirit manifested by the friends and adherents of the Boston company, that editorials were written condemning the manner in which said company was defeated. These false rumors caused the referee, Major Egan, U. S. A., to write the following letter:

WEST POINT, N. Y., *July* 31, 1868.

Colonel :—I see in some of the papers of to-day that surprise is expressed at the decision of the drill of yesterday, and I hasten (although a stranger till yesterday to you and your officers) to give you an account of that decision.

Both judges, the one on the part of your company and the one on the part of the company from Boston, as they could not agree, left the decision to me, and I gave the flag to the company of your regiment for the following reasons:

In every part of the drill, save the manual of arms, the company of your regiment followed the tactics faithfully and excelled the contesting company. The marching, manœuvring, and steadiness in carrying arms, time of step, dress and attention of the men, were all better, and throughout the drill there was an honest adherence to tactics that the other company did not follow.

Capt. Finan's company excelled the one of your regiment in the manual, but not enough to counterbalance its deficiencies in other respects.

I see, also, there is an accusation of foul play. I certainly did not see any of it, though I faithfully took notice of everything. The ground was obstructed *often* during the drill of your company, and *once* during the drill of Capt. Finan's company. He complained of it, and I had the drill stopped at once, till abundance of space was cleared for him; and, from the shouts of admiration, I am confident that the friends of Capt. Finan's company obstructed the drill.

I saw no disposition on the part of the spectators to discourage either company; nor was there cause for either company to be discouraged, and every assertion to the contrary is false.

Respectfully, JOHN EGAN,
Captain Infantry and Brevet Major.

To Col. JOHN WARD, Commanding Twelfth Infantry.

Immediately thereafter, a leading journal of New York, spoke of the affair in the language following, which is as amusing as it is truthful :

THE LATE CHAMPION DRILL.—One would suppose, from the erratic editorials and curious correspondence inserted in one of our "leading dailies" (whose amusing accounts of the National Guard often provoke smiles and laughter among military men), that the so-called champions of Massachusetts had been fairly champed and mashed up while on a recent visit to this city; and furthermore, that if one or two wonderfully historic sheets may be believed, or their friends in this city are entitled to the least credence, Company I, Ninth Regiment, Massachusetts Volunteer Militia (more familiarly known as the Montgomery Guard of Boston), must be the best-abused company that ever came upon a visit to this city.

Either these journals, which seek to make capital or create talk from this matter, are acting maliciously or in ignorance, is certain, for the reason that Company E, Twelfth Infantry, N.*G. S. N. Y., not only won their honors, but are fairly entitled to the same, they having given evidence of superior drill and manœuvring, although not so perfect in the manual. While lamenting with our cotemporaries that the police arrangements at Tompkins Square were so bad, we, nevertheless, must object to the ridiculous remarks and insane criticism which has been attached to this affair.

We think that the Boston Company will admit that the Sixty-Ninth Regiment, Infantry, of New York, having not the slightest interest in the contest, at considerable expense to themselves, and with a generosity characteristic of the race from which they sprung, took good care of them while here; and also that the Twelfth Regiment (including even their rivals of Company E) did all that was possible to make them feel at home. They fairly lost the flag, and could not have won it had Tompkins Square been twice as large as it is.

For the Captain of the defeated company to write a critical communication to the referee is not only in exceedingly bad taste, but to publish it, accompanied by a second challenge, is worse. Its only effect, perhaps, will be to induce more negro minstrels to present fresh flags to the much-wronged Montgomery Guard—a company that evidently came to New York to make a few stamps or establish a brilliant reputation. Had their over-anxious friends not crowded about the company so much, swinging their greenbacks in the face of every New Yorker upon the ground, and acted so noisily, probably the Massachusetts champions might have been less nervous, taken the right sort of a step, and committed less mistakes than they did; but this was no fault of the Twelfth Regiment boys, who knew the difficult task they had in hand, and steadily performed it. As upon the occasion of a match between a celebrated drum corps of this city and that of this same Twelfth Regiment, in which the latter were pronounced to be the victors, there was no fancy work—no flummery—nothing to awaken applause. They won in the same manner that Company E did, by a faithful compliance with the book and in strict accordance with the rules of the agreement.

There is no doubt that Company I, Ninth Regiment, Massachusetts Volunteer Militia, is (to use a Yankee phrase) "a right smart company," and has often astonished the "Bosting folks" with its dashing drill. But when they came to New York in the expectation of bluffing its entire citizen soldiery, they made one very large mistake; and we fancy that if Company E, of the Twelfth, had not taken the starch out of their exceedingly stiff and high collars, some other unpretending squad of our National Guard boys would have done it for them, in a decent and quiet manner. The winning of flags in country villages and the wearing of frightful-looking Zouave costumes do not constitute champion companies, and people not understanding military matters may be apt to confound the meretricious with the meritorious. Our desire is simply to do justice to both sides. We shall, therefore, in conclusion, simply pick out a portion of the drill, and after upsetting the false statements (we shall not call it criticism) of some of the impudent organs of the New York and Boston press, inform them how and why it is that the Montgomery Guard is so superior in their manual to Company E, Twelfth Regiment, Infantry, N. G., and also that their celerity in the handling of the piece is no drawback.

Our space does not enable us to quote military authority in full; but those anxious to sift things down to a right understanding can safely conclude that such persons or critics as assert that "Capt.

Finan's men did remarkably well, but that their manual was too quick," are in error. There is no specified time fixed for the execution of the manual; but it is distinctly stated, in all military works, that it shall be executed "briskly." We take this to mean quick time, as is implied in Scott, paragraphs 159, 408, and 474; Hardee, 129, 323; Casey, 136, 332; and Upton, 104, 148, 323, and 455. The quickness in the execution of the manual by the Montgomery Guard is not in any way against them, as the "ninetieth part of a minute" is not continuously called for in the several motions, and does not govern the time always. We must, therefore, award the palm for superiority in the handling of the musket to the Boston Company; but for marching and manœuvring, the prize must be given to Company E, Twelfth Infantry, N. G. S. N. Y. It remains to be seen if the latter can retain their laurels.

The aforesaid drill, its circumstances and results, are mentioned solely with the view to manifest that competitive drills excite in military bodies a laudable ambition to excel. If properly conducted, are they not calculated to render the competing parties proficients in the art of infantry warfare? The idea, that such drills beget ill feeling between our military bodies, is erroneous. Any regiment which would shrink from a challenge to drill for a prize at a competitive drill, merely because a little dissatisfaction might follow, would probably flee from the enemy in time of war.

Henry M. Karples enlisted in Company E, Twelfth N. Y. M., April 19, 1861. Served with his company and regiment until mustered out in August, 1861. Was commissioned a First Lieutenant in the Fifty-Second N. Y. V. March 10, 1862. Served with his regiment in the peninsular campaign, the seven days' battles before Richmond, second Bull Run, South Mountain, Antietam, Fredericksburg, and the last fight of the rebellion before Petersburg. He was promoted through the several grades, to that of Colonel of his regiment; and while leading his regiment, was several times severely wounded. He is now in the army, with the rank of First Lieutenant in the Thirty-Sixth Infantry. Col. Karples is an officer of no mean ability, lacks none of the requisites that make the soldier, is kind to inferiors, re spectful and obedient to superiors, and has an entire disregard of personal danger.

James W. Parks enlisted in Company E, Twelfth N. Y. M., April 19, 1861. Served with his company and regiment until their return to New York, in August, 1861. Upon being discharged, he went to New Hampshire. Was offered and accepted the commission of Second Lieutenant in the Fifth N. H. V. He participated with his regiment in the battles before Richmond, second Bull Run, South Mountain, and Antietam. Was wounded severely in the head at Fair Oaks, June 1, 1862, and in the hip at Antietam, September 17, 1862, after which he was transferred to the Veteran Reserve Corps, with the rank of First Lieutenant (having previously attained this rank in the Fifth N. H. V.); and when the army was put on a peace footing, he was honorably discharged.

Isaac Blauvelt enlisted in Company E, Twelfth N. Y. M., and served with his regiment until the same was mustered out, although before the expiration of his term of enlistment he was commissioned First Lieutenant in the Seventeenth N. Y. V. Upon his return to New York with the Twelfth he immediately joined the Seventeenth, and with it went to meet the enemy, and participated in all the engagements on the peninsula, as well as that of second Bull Run, where he fell leading his men, and "with his face toward the foe." He had previous to his death attained the rank of Captain. No honors could be paid him there. A hasty ditch, a few shovelfulls of dirt, and amid the thunder of rebel guns, Capt. Blauvelt was buried. A firm friend, a fearless soldier, he fills an unknown grave; yet his memory is kept green. E Company has no brighter example to emulate, nor more honored name upon its roll, than that of Capt. Isaac Blauvelt. Peace to his ashes.

Capt. Robert McAffee, at present in command of E Company, is considered the handsomest and most soldier-like officer in the First Brigade. As an instructing officer, he is equal to any in the Division. No further proof of this need be presented, than the admirable display of his company during the late competitive drill in Tompkins Square. The skill and proficiency manifested by his corps in said drill are in a great measure attributable to the intelligence and perseverance of Capt. McAffee. Like his brother (the Lieutenant Colonel of the Twelfth), he has a clear, powerful, and sonorous voice, which can be distinctly heard whenever he utters a command.

4

PRESENT MEMBERS OF E COMPANY.

COMMISSIONED OFFICERS.

Date of Commission.
Captain, Robert McAffee................Feb. 13, 1867.
First Lieutenant, Wm. H. Smith...........   "   "
Second Lieutenant, James F. McCuen.......   "   "

DRUMMERS.

Date of Certificate.
John Gunn...........................May 1, 1868.
James V. B. Covey....................Oct. 2,   "

SERGEANTS.

Date of Warrant.
First Sergeant, Thomas G. Seely..........Oct. 4, 1867.
Second Sergeant, Wm. J. Lodge...........Apr. 5,   "
Third Sergeant, Stephen Bateman..........Feb. 1,   "
Fourth Sergeant, Benjamin Plumb.........Dec. 7,   "
Fifth Sergeant, John Williams............Oct. 4,   "

CORPORALS.

Henry B. Lambert.....................May 6, 1864.
James Ross...........................Feb. 1, 1867.

PRIVATES.

Date of Certificate.
Abel Augustus.......................May 22, 1868.
Armstrong, Wm. H....................Apr. 29, 1862.
Allen, William ....Feb. 2, 1866.
Allen, Julian.......................Sept. 28, "
Blake, John.........................Feb. 19, 1864.
Cook, Joseph........................Feb. 13,   "
Clarke, Henry H.....................Mar. 31, 1865.
Chamberlain, Chas. W................Aug. 16, 1867.
Drummond, R. B......................Oct. 30, 1868.
Doerle, John J......................May 29,   "
Doerle, Philip...................... " 22,   "
Dowd, Robert........................Feb. 8, 1867.
Ezekiel, Moses......................July 23, 1866.
French, Wm. C.......................Mar. 18, 1864.
Gaddis, David.......................July 1,   "
Garbrandt, Isaac W..................May 11, 1866.

Ganun, Alfred M............................Nov. 3, 1865.
Gault, James..............................Sept. 2, 1864.
Gamble, John..............................Apr. 1, "
Hammond, Chas. N..........................May 25, 1865.
Hearsey, G. H.............................Dec. 1, "
Harris, Mark..............................Nov. 3, "
Jackson, James............................Apr. 29, 1862.
Jackson, Wm. J............................Feb. 3, 1865.
Lawrence, Joseph..........................Apr. 10, 1863.
Leonard, Terance..........................July 6, 1866.
Lynch, Thomas P...........................Oct. 23, 1868.
Moulton, Chas. F..........................Oct. 30, "
McAffee, William..........................June 10, "
McCuen, William...........................Apr. 13, 1866.
McMullen, Oliver..........................Feb. 2, "
Newell, John..............................Feb. 5, 1864.
Rowan, George (armorer)...................May 3, 1867.
Rhinehardt, James.........................Mar. 11, "
Shephard, Charles.........................May 12, 1865.
Scott, Samuel............................. " 25, "
Silvia, Theodore V........................Sept. 8, "
Stivers, Jerome........................... " 16, "
Stivers, G. E. W.......................... " 8, "
Veitch, F. A..............................May 13, 1864.
Walsh, Robert.............................June 8, 1866.
Waldron, Walter H.........................Mar. 24, 1865.
Wright, Wm. B.............................Apr. 22, 1864.
Wood, Wm. H...............................Nov. 25, "

F Company.

The original title of this corps, was "Lafayette Fusileers." Its first commandant, Capt. French. It left New York, with the Regiment, in 1861, commanded by

Captain, James Cromie.
First Lieutenant, Wm. Dyott.
Second Lieutenant, Henry Rowley.

Previous to the rebellion, this company had for its Captains such eminent men as William G. Ward, now General of the First Brigade, N. G. S. N. Y.

James Cromie, whose gallantry in the late war obtained for him the position of Major in the U. S. A.

John Ward, the excellent Colonel, commanding the Regiment.

During the first year of the war, Lieut. Emery Upton was detailed as instructor of this Company. Of the glory which Lieut. Barlow's career shed, not only on this corps, but upon the Regiment, mention is made in the pages preceding.

Capt. Milnor Imlay, at present in command of F Company, was actively engaged during the first year of the war in the organization and drilling of companies for the field. In 1862, he joined I Company, Seventh Regiment, and served with it in the field and in the city during the riots of 1863. After his return from Maryland in 1865, he was elected Second Lieutenant of this corps. On the 24th of January, 1866, he was chosen Captain, vice Capt. John Ward, promoted Major. From the date of Capt. Imlay's appointment as Second Lieutenant till the time when he was elected to command, about one year, he brought into the company twenty first-class recruits, for which Capt. Ward presented him with a gold medal. In the Board of Officers of the Twelfth

Regiment, Capt. Imlay is respected and admired. During the six years that have elapsed since his connection with the Twelfth, he was never summoned before the Regimental Court Martial, nor has he missed a company meeting or drill. On the 30th of September, 1868, he and Capt. John Fahnestock, of Company K, Twelfth Regiment, prepared an excursion, of which the following was the programme:

EXCURSION TO NEW HAVEN.

BATTALION F AND K CO'S, 12TH REGT., N. G. S. N. Y., }
NEW YORK, *September* 30, 1868. }

The arrangements for this excursion are as follows:
On the evening of Tuesday, October 13th, the Battalion, accompanied by Regimental Band and Drum Corps, will leave New York at eleven o'clock, on steamboat Elm City, arriving in New Haven at six o'clock the next morning.

The Battalion will be received and escorted to quarters (Tontine Hall), by the Second Regiment, Connecticut Militia.

At ten o'clock A. M., the Battalion will be welcomed to the city and reviewed by the Mayor and Common Council.

At three o'clock P. M., a joint parade with the Second Regiment, C. M., will take place through the principal streets, to be followed by a formal review by His Excellency Governor English and his Staff, in full uniform.

In the evening a Promenade Concert, in aid of the New Haven Orphan Asylum, will be given at Music Hall, by the Regimental Band and Drum Corps, at which Governor English and Staff will be present.

The next day, October 15th, will be given wholly to enjoyment, in the form of a Grand Clam Bake and Picnic at Sabin Rock, which will be the occasion of a social reunion of the members of the Battalion, and the Second C. M.

At eleven o'clock in the evening the Battalion will embark for home, arriving Friday morning at six o'clock, thus consummating, it can be safely said, the most enjoyable military excursion of the season.

A joint meeting of F and K Companies to make final arrangements, and to transact all incidental business, will be held at the Regimental Armory, on Wednesday evening next, October 7th at eight o'clock.

All persons designing to take part in the excursion are earnestly requested to be present at this meeting.

Members of other companies of the Regiment are specially invited to join with us.

The Regular Monthly Meetings of F and K Companies are hereby postponed until further notice.

CAPT. MILNOR IMLAY, F Company.
CAPT. JOHN FAHNESTOCK, K Company.

The *Army and Navy Journal* speaks thus of the excursion :

EXCURSION OF COMPANIES F AND K, TWELFTH REGIMENT.—On Tuesday evening, October 15th, Companies F and K, of the Twelfth Regiment, left New York, in the steamer Elm City, on an excursion to New Haven. The companies on this occasion paraded about 100 strong, including the regimental band and a drum corps of eight pieces, and were under the command of Capt. Milnor Imlay. The following officers accompanied the excursion : Lieut. Whitenack (Company K), acting Adjutant; Capt. Fahnestock and Lieut. Donald, Company K, and Lieut. Victor Herb and Lieut. Healy, of Company F. The steamer left the wharf foot of Peck Slip at eleven o'clock P. M., arriving at her destination at about five o'clock A. M. Between six and seven o'clock a delegation consisting of Lieut. Pardee, and several members of Company E, Second Connecticut, came on board the steamer and gave the excursionists an informal but hearty welcome.

At about seven o'clock the Battalion of the Twelfth formed on the steamboat wharf, and marched to the armory of the Light Guard (Company E), Second Connecticut, where they stacked their arms. The men were then dismissed and preceeded to the Tontine Hotel for breakfast, making this hotel their headquarters during their stay in the city. The weather not proving propitious the parade was postponed until the afternoon. It was some considerable time after the appointed time before the escorting companies made their appearance. When they finally did arrive at Chapel Street, where the companies of the Twelth were drawn up, the usual formalities were gone through with; after which the march was at once commenced. The column was composed of the officers of the staff of Gen. Russel, commanding Connecticut National Guard, a delegation of the officers of the Second Connecticut Infantry ; a squadron of the Governor's Guard in column of platoons, Major Merwin commanding; four companies of the Second Connecticut Infantry, Major S. R. Smith commanding, and finally the battalion of the Twelfth Regiment.

The Governor's Guard is uniformed in gray, and was on this occasion accompanied by their band. The appearance of this body of mounted men was highly creditable, and will compare favorably with any of our New York Cavalry. The infantry was preceded by Felsbury's Band, the Sarsfield Guard, Capt. Joseph H. Keefe, having the right of the line. This company paraded in single rank, and made a fine appearance, wearing a full dress uniform, similar to that recently adopted by the Ninth New York National Guard, which has been presented to the Guard by the citizens of New Haven. The second company in line also paraded in single rank, but, with the rest of the regiment, wore the ordinary State uniform. The rest of the companies paraded in two ranks and marched well.

Upon their arrival at "The Green," the troops were reviewed by Governor English, Mayor Sperry, and several members of the Governor's staff and other officials, all in citizens' clothes. Major Smith was in command at the review. At the conclusion of the review they made a somewhat extended march through the principal streets of the city. At the review and on the march the companies of the Twelfth made a very good appearance, excelling in their marching, etc., most of the Connecticut infantry which paraded with them. At the conclusion of the march a dress parade was gone through with, the ceremony being concluded with a prayer by the chaplain of the Second Connecticut.

In the evening a promenade concert was given at Music Hall by the band of the Twelfth Regiment, under the leadership of Bandmaster Otto. This concert was given for the benefit of the Soldiers' Orphan Asylum, of New Haven. Governor English and staff, Mayor Sperry, and other officials, were present, and the concert, as well as the hop which followed it, were highly enjoyable. The following day, Thursday, was not favorable to a grand excursion to Sabin Rock, and it was accordingly postponed, although quite a number of the Twelfth visited the Rock in the afternoon, and had a pleasant time there. In the evening the Battalion of the Twelfth, under the escort of the Light Guard and the Sarsfield Guard, proceeded to the steamboat Continental, stopping on their way to serenade Governor English, who acknowledged the compliment by a short speech.

The trip home was without incident. The excursionists arrived in New York on Friday morning. The members of the Light Guard and the Sarsfield Guard did all in their power to make the visit of the Battalion to New Haven a pleasant one. The men of the Twelfth behaved themselves with great propriety and decorum.

PRESENT MEMBERS OF F COMPANY.

COMMISSIONED OFFICERS.

	Date of Commission.
Captain, Milnor Imlay	Feb. 18, 1866.
First Lieutenant, Victor Herb	Apr. 4, 1867.
Second Lieutenant, Samuel V. Healey	" "

DRUMMERS.

	Date of Certificate.
Eugene Mazgochi	Oct. 1, 1866.
Michael Daly	Oct. 10, 1867.

SERGEANTS.

	Date of Warrant.
First Sergeant, Morris Duckworth	Apr. 1, 1868.
Second Sergeant, Jacob Burkhardt	Nov. 7, 1867.
Third Sergeant, Chas. Earwicker	Feb. 5, 1868.
Fourth Sergeant, John A. McGee	Nov. 7, 1867.
Fifth Sergeant, John W. James	June 3, 1868.

CORPORALS.

Robert Carlton	Nov. 7, 1867.
Richard B. Eason	" "
Charles P. Smith	" "
Edward H. Healy	May 6, 1868.
Morris Gordon	" "

PRIVATES.

	Date of Certificate.
Berkley, William	Feb. 1, 1860.
Blatz, Joseph	Jan. 6, 1864.
Barnes, Leveret	Oct. 14, 1865.
Consall, John W	Mar. 2, 1864.
Clear, Martin	Aug. 5, 1868.
Calhoun, Alonzo	Mar. 7, 1864.
Day, Wm. L	" 15, 1865.
Devoe, Frederick	" 7, 1866.
Evers, David	May 23, "
Eason, John V	" 9, "
Ellis, John H	Jan. 6, 1861.
Granger, William	Apr. 1, 1863.
Granger, Samuel	Nov. 19, 1862.

TWELFTH INFANTRY.

Iker, Frederick..........................July 3, 1860.
Ivans, Wm. D..........................Oct. 4, 1865.
Kearney, John..........................Oct. 23, 1867.
Keyes, William.........................Jan. 9,   "
Labrie, J..............................Dec. 8, 1865.
Menair, James..........................Oct. 4,   "
O'Neil, John...........................May 27, 1866.
Owens, Chas. E......................... " 23,   "
Palmer, James S........................Oct. 4, 1865.
Rose, Warren H.........................Jan. 22, 1868.
Robson, John J.........................Oct. 4, 1865.
Riley, John............................May 4, 1864.
Roberts, Wm. J.........................Feb. 14, 1866.
Sloan, William.........................Apr. 2, 1862.
Samuels, George........................July 25, 1866.
Schopper, Henry........................May 4, 1864.
Sweeten, Alexander.....................Feb. 16, 1865.
Taylor, George......................... "   5, 1866.
Tucker, S. W...........................Oct. 4, 1865.
Van Worden, J. W.......................July 11, 1866.
Weaber, Arnold.........................Oct. 17,   "
Weaver, Benjamin, jr...................July 4,   "
Wier, Samuel...........................Jan. 24,   "
Young, Robert II.......................Apr. 11, 1861.

4*

G COMPANY.

"Independence Guard" is the title which this corps bore in 1847; and in addition to its letter, still bears its original beautiful name.

Capt. Cairns was its first commandant.

The following ex-members of Company G are worthy of mention:

Capt. Jas. A. Boyle, present proprietor of Knickerbocker Cottage, and former commandant of Company G, has a record of which this corps and the whole Regiment are proud. He is a gentleman naturally genial, generous, and brave. An account of his conduct during the rebellion would be inserted here, were it not that he abhors publishing deeds of duty, however valiantly performed. Suffice it to say, that Capt. Boyle's character, both as a citizen and a soldier, is a model worthy of imitation.

First Lieut. W. W. Chamberlain, and Second Lieut. J. A. Ritoul, also rendered efficient service.

Lieut. Chamberlain, for his bravery, was transferred to the United States Regular Army, with full commission as Lieutenant, and was killed at a skirmish at the second battle of Bull Run.

T. H. Brown fought in twelve of the great Virginia battles, was severely wounded, and is now a Captain in the Regular Army.

Charles Lyon, for distinguished gallantry at Fredericksburg, was made an aid on Gen. Butler's staff.

S. A. Jenett was promoted as Major in the Army of the Cumberland, but was slain at Shiloh.

Brevet Brig. Gen. F. T. Locke, of whom previous mention has been made, was a member of this corps.

Brigade Inspector Gilon.

Edward Gilon joined Company G on the 7th of August, 1860, as a private. In 1861 he was appointed Corporal, and occupied said position till the end of that year's campaign. In September of the latter year he was elected First Sergeant. He participated with the company in the campaigns of 1863. On the 17th of January, 1865, he was elected First Lieutenant of this corps; and on the 7th of the following April, elected Captain. This office he filled with great benefit and honor to the company till the 29th of April, 1867. On the day last mentioned, he received from Brig. Gen. W. G. Ward the appointment of Inspector of the First Brigade Infantry, with rank of Major. This important position he fills with marked distinction.

When Capt. Gilon retired from Company G, he left it in a prosperous condition. Gen. Ward manifested excellent judgment and discernment in appointing Capt. Gilon as Brigade Inspector. He is quick, courteous, and intelligent.

Patrick McGrain, now an active member of this corps, went through the war with the gallant Sixty-Ninth N. Y. M.

Cornelius Evans served with this corps in 1863, and afterward became an officer in the Fifty-First N. Y. V.

Corporal David Watson distinguished himself in the company's term of service in 1863. He served also with the Fifty-First Regiment during the war, and was made a line officer.

Sergt. Jas. C. Angus fought at Harper's Ferry in 1862, and served three years with the One Hundred and Sixty-Fifth N. Y. S. M.

Sergt. Bernard McGowan, a gallant young officer, served with distinction in the last named regiment.

Second Lieut. E. S. Conklin, a brave officer, participated in the severest battles of 1865. He is at present in the company.

First Lieut. Richard E. Jones, an officer of rare courage, distinguished himself at the battle of Harper's Ferry, and during the Pennsylvania battles.

Capt. Charles J. McGowan is one of the most active and intelligent officers in the National Guard. He served with the Regiment in 1861. Since then he has filled, in an honorable manner, an important position in the United States Ordnance Department. He commands Company G. As a tactician, Capt. McGowan ranks among the first. His company, in point of drill and discipline, is second to none in the First Division.

PRESENT MEMBERS OF G COMPANY.

COMMISSIONED OFFICERS.
Date of Commission.

Captain, Chas. J. McGowan..............June 26, 1867.
First Lieutenant, R. E. Jones............ "   "
Second Lieutenant, Egbert S. Conkling.....Jan. 4, 1868.

DRUMMERS.
Date of Certificate.

Cornelius Evans........................Nov. 13, 1862.
William Parker........................Sept. 10, 1867.

SERGEANTS.
Date of Warrant.

First Sergeant, Wm. H. Brown...........Jan. 21, 1868.
Second Sergeant, Samuel White........... "   "
Third Sergeant, James C. Angus.........Apr. 7, 1865.
Fourth Sergeant, Jacob Haring..........Sept. 1, 1868.
Fifth Sergeant, ——— ——— .... ———

CORPORALS.

David Watson..........................June 12, 1866.
John W. Berrian.......................Aug. 6, 1867.
Frank D. Baker........................Sept. 1. 1868.
William McPherson..................... "   "

PRIVATES.
Date of Certificate.

Ackerman, D. H........................Aug. 7, 1866.
Blanck, Henry.........................Oct. 2,   "
Campbell, R. H........................May 12, 1868.
Foster, John..........................Mar. 3,   "
Finnigan, Patrick H...................Apr. 2, 1867.
Goeller, C. F.........................Aug. 7, 1866.
Heintz, Emile H.......................July 19, 1865.
Hoffman, George.......................June 7, 1864.
Jeens, Wm. H..........................Oct. 14, 1865.
Keyser, George W......................Apr. 7, 1868.
Keating, Francis......................Dec. 4, 1867.
McGowan, Bernard......................July 3, 1866.
McGrain, Patrick......................Dec. 4, 1866.
Mitchell, W. B........................Apr. 12, 1864.

HONORARY ROLL OF THE

Robertson, A. J..........................July 2, 1867.
Rothwell, John..........................Aug. 7, 1866.
Rabell, Charles.......................... "   "   "
Ryberg, Frank H........................May 1,   "
Ryberg, Randolph C....................Apr. 7, 1862.
Ryberg, Frederick T....................Oct. 27, "
Shiel, John.............................Aug. 20, 1861.
Schreyer, William......................Apr. 2, 1867.
Teller, Charles..........................Feb. 9, 1864.
Von Grichton, H.......................Oct. 3, 1865.
Wheeler, Alonzo........................Aug. 3, "
Walker, John E......................... "   7, 1866.
White, Wm. S..........................July 7, 1868.
Wintrich, Peter.........................Sept. 1, "

H Company.

"Baxter Blues" was the original name of Company H, under command of Capt. Waterbury.

In 1861, when this company entered on its first campaign, it had for its officers:

Captain, Wm. H. McCormack.
First Lieutenant, Ezekiel Vance.
Second Lieutenant, D. G. McKelric.

The celebrated Gen. Sweeney, who distinguished himself, not only in the Mexican war, but also in the war for the preservation of the Union, was an active member of this corps.

M. I. Reynolds, an old member of H Company, went from New York to Illinois in 1864, joined the Eighty-Sixth Illinois as First Lieutenant, went with it to the seat of war, and returned as Major. He had, at one time, charge of the rebel prisoners confined in Chicago.

Bernard Ryan, after leaving the Company with an honorable record, removed to Rochester, N. Y., and raised a company of ninety-six men, of whom he was elected Captain. He joined the Eighty-Ninth N. Y. S. M., and was slain before Petersburg.

Charles Blauvelt, Member of Assembly from the Fifth District of New York, is an ex-officer of this corps. He served with the Regiment during the campaigns of 1862, and was taken prisoner at Harper's Ferry.

John A. Dougan, the celebrated hatter, cor. of Nassau and Ann Streets, New York, is an ex-officer of H. Company. During the rebellion he spent large sums of money from his private fortune to recruit and equip companies for the Union Army. And now, "when the cruel war is over," he always extends a helping hand to the maimed soldiers that are to be found everywhere, imploring the people's pittance. He is in fact one of those high-minded, public spirited citizens, whose name the Twelfth Regiment may well be proud to inscribe on its Honorary Roll.

H. C. Coleman left the Company about the same time, as the last named party. He raised a company in Pittsford, N. Y. Said company was called the "Coleman Guard," and was placed as a guard over the prisoners at Elmira.

Capt. George Teets, present commandant of H Company, is a gentleman of energy and ability. Like every genuine officer, he duly estimates the importance of the duties of his position. Hence he performs them in an exact and punctual manner. As a necessary consequence, the members of his corps are noted for their strict observance of duty.

PRESENT MEMBERS OF H COMPANY.

COMMISSIONED OFFICERS.
Date of Commission.
Captain, George Toets..................Oct. 28, 1866.
First Lieutenant, —— —— ....
Second Lieutenant, John C. Moore.........Jan. 4, 1868.

DRUMMERS.
Date of Certificate.
John McNulty.......................Oct. 2, 1866.
John Sheehan........................ "   "

SERGEANTS.
Date of Warrant.
First Sergeant, D. G. McKelvey..........Feb. 6, 1867.
Second Sergeant, Thomas Hoban..........May 28, "
Third Sergeant, John Noble.............Nov. 12, "
Fourth Sergeant, Alex. N. Hourier........Sept. 22, 1868.
Fifth Sergeant, Henry F. Banks...........   "   "

CORPORALS.
William Chittenden.....................Feb. 10, 1868.
William Graham........................Feb. 9, 1865.
Charles Clifford.......................Sept. 22, 1868.
Peter W. Hennessy....................   "   "

PRIVATES.
Date of Certificate.
Bruner, Otto............................Sept. 1, 1868.
Brown, George........................ "   6, 1864.
Connor, Thomas........................Feb. 8, 1864.
Coffman, Wm. J........................Jan. 21, 1868.
Chambers, Samuel......................Oct. 18, 1862.
Coffee, John...........................Sept. 4, 1866.
Darragh, Thomas.......................Oct. 1, 1862.
Douglas, Charles.......................Sept. 22, 1868.
Ellis, Henry S.........................Feb. 12, 1861.
Fehey, James H........................Dec. 17, 1867.
Hope, Walter..........................Sept. 27, 1868.
Heron, John V.........................Jan. 18, 1862.
Hageman, J. B........................May 24, 1865.

Harrison, Luke........................Nov. 14, 1866.
Joice, John...........................May 2, 1865.
McLaughlin H. ....Jan. 12, 1866.
Mulry, Lawrence......................Mar. 11, 1862.
Mellish, Henry....................... " 4, 1862.
Parr, Robert.........................May 2, 1865.
Ryer, Moses H......................Sept. 26, 1867.
Ray, John J.........................Apr. 23, "
Robinson, Henry C...................Oct. 9, 1865.
Reynolds, Edward D.................Apr. 23, 1867.
Stinson, Thomas....................Jan. 18, 1860.
Turner, Hugh.......................Mar. 14, 1862.
Zimmerman, George.................. " 22, 1864.

I COMPANY.

This corps was organized as the Sixth Company of the Twenty-Seventh Regiment, N. G., in January, 1825, under command of L. W. Stearns.

On the 20th of November, 1833, Thomas Postly, being Captain, the company passed a resolution to petition Governor Marcy for a transfer, as a " flank company," to the Eighth Regiment Light Infantry. On the 30th day of the following month, the company adopted the title of " National Grays," which they retained till April 4, 1861, when they were transferred to and became I Company in the Twelfth Regiment. Even now, the corps occasionally displays its pristine name.

Between the years 1845 and 1861, Company I was known as belonging to the Tenth and Twenty-Third Regiments.

On the 22d of February, 1854, the " Grays," by invitation, visited Buffalo, to join in the celebration of Washington's Birthday. They were the first company from the city of New York to visit Syracuse, Rochester, Buffalo, and Niagara Falls.

Brevet Col. Jacob Raynor was commandant of this corps, for more than twenty years, and did much to make it what it is, a first-class company. He was elected on the 28th of March, 1836.

With the balance of the battalion, Company I went to the seat of war in 1861. During the campaign of the first three months its commissioned officers were :

Captain, Wm. Raynor.
First Lieutenant, H. R. Mackay.
Second Lieutenant, L. R. Bingham.
Second Lieut., E. Fisher (killed in U. S. service).

Capt. Acorn, who commanded this corps at Harper's Ferry, in 1862, was praised in General Orders for meritorious and gallant conduct. His Lieutenant, John S.

Ellison also displayed admirable coolness and bravery. Lieutenant Ellison was afterward commissioned as Captain of the Twelfth New York Cavalry, stationed in North Carolina. Served as Lieutenant Colonel of the Second North Carolina Cavalry, and engaged in several severe engagements. He is an officer of remarkable courage and ability. He has in his possession testimonials from some of the most prominent Generals of the Union Army, among them General Wessel of the Regular Army.

The most notorious member of I Company during its term of service in 1861, was Boston Corbit. While doing duty as a private, he called a superior officer to order for using words that were not purely evangelical. The officer thus reprimanded in presence of his command, for the sake of discipline, ordered Boston to enter on a spiritual retreat in the Guard House. Corbit, however, was soon released, feeling much stronger in spirit than in the flesh. And the next great and notorious act of his, that the world heard of (let those praise it who will), was the shooting of John Wilkes Booth.

Boston Corbit, with all his eccentricities in the field, his burning zeal for the conversion of sinners, and his boisterousness in prayer meetings, is a sincere Christian, and a brave man.

Surgeon Weir, of whom previous mention is made, was a private in this company in 1861.

Col. Thompson, of the Twenty-Second Kentucky Volunteers, was at one time a private in this company. He fought in sixteen battles, was wounded twelve different times. He is now in the Regular army.

Sergt. Lord, of this corps, joined a New Hampshire regiment in 1863. His gallant conduct caused his promotion to the position of Major. He is in the United States Cavalry, stationed at Carson City.

Brig. Gen. Hall, after having served two years in Company I as a private, removed to Wisconsin, raised a regiment, went to the Army of the Cumberland, and, by incomparable bravery, rose to the rank of Brigadier General. At present he is silver-mining in Colorado.

Samuel H. Crook, jr. This young gentleman is a private in I Company, though he graduated with honors at Tarrytown Military Academy. He has had several opportunities of promotion, but like Hon. Hannibal Hamlin, ex-Vice-President, he deems it honorable to bear arms even as a private in the National Guard.

Samuel H. Crook, jr., belongs to a family thoroughly republican. His father, S. H. Crook, senior, the courteous proprietor of the well-known hotel on Chatham Street, heartily approves, and is proud of the genuine American spirit manifested by his son.

Major Sherman went with this company to the seat of war in 1862, as a private, and is now in the Regular Army, stationed at Santa Fe. He is related to Lieut. Gen. Sherman.

Lieut. Briggs, who was slain at the battle of Fredericksburg, served as a private in this corps in 1861.

Col. Clark, who commanded the Fifth Missouri Volunteers at the battle of Wilson's Creek, held the position of Corporal in I Company previous to the rebellion.

Lieut. Henry B. Wilson, joined I Company in the month of April, 1861, and served as a private during the campaigns of that year. In 1862 he was chosen Sergeant, and after displaying much bravery, was taken prisoner at Harper's Ferry. During the term of service of 1863, he acted as Second Sergeant, and subsequently received the appointment of Sergeant Major. Recently he was unanimously elected Second Lieutenant, which position he occupies with distinction.

Lieut. John E. Dowley joined I Company on the 20th of April, 1861, and served with the Regiment during its "war campaigns." Prompt obedience and unvarying punctuality are among the distinguishing traits of his character. During the riots of 1863, he was elected Second Lieutenant of this corps. He filled this office with credit till August, 1867, when he was chosen to fill the position of First Lieutenant. He was nominated for the Captaincy, but declined in favor of J. H.

French, the present courteous commander. Among the members of Company I, he is respected and esteemed. At the expiration of his seven years term of service, October 15, 1868, they manifested their esteem by presenting him with a splendid gold watch. He is at present Deputy United States Marshal under Gen. Barlow.

Capt. John H. French joined Company I in October, 1862. He served in all the "non-com." grades. In 1863, he went with the Regiment through the Pennsylvania campaigns, and gave many tokens of his military skill and daring. He pays special attention to his military duties, hence everything appertaining to his office is in admirable order. He is very exact about the character and social standing of all parties seeking admission to membership in his corps, consequently the company is composed of respectable young gentlemen. Capt. French, too, offers valuable presents to parties bringing acceptable recruits. Not long ago, he gave to the company a rich gold medal to be worn by the member who labors most assiduously to increase the ranks. While I Company is commanded by Capt. French it will prosper.

PRESENT MEMBERS OF I COMPANY.

COMMISSIONED OFFICERS.

Date of Commission.
Captain, John H. French.................Nov. 23, 1867.
First Lieutenant, John F. Dowley..........July 26, "
Second Lieutenant, Henry B. Wilson........Nov. 23, "

DRUMMERS.

Date of Certificate.
William Irving..........................Sept. 20, 1867.
Richard McKay..........................April 23, 1868.

SERGEANTS.

Date of Warrant.
First Sergeant, Joseph M. Schenck........Aug. 15, 1867.
Second Sergeant, Wm. H. Schwalbic........Dec. 19, "
Third Sergeant, Edward Fackner...........Nov. 21, "
Fourth Sergeant, Henry O. Storms.........Aug. 27, 1868.
Fifth Sergeant, Wm. B. Kauth.............Jan.   1869.

CORPORALS.

George Baumgartner.....................Aug. 15, 1867.
John H. Anderson....................... "   27, 1868.
Philip Baker........................... "   22, "
Felix J. O'Neil........................ "   27, 1867.

PRIVATES.

Date of Certificate.
Acorn, Henry...........................Oct. 30, 1862.
Bowman, John...........................May 10, 1866.
Baker, William H. H....................Sept. 17, 1863.
Briggs, Theo. B........................March 19, "
Crook, S. H., Jr., (Grad. of Tarryt'n Mil. A.), Oct. 1, 1868.
Cromwell, George....................... " 30, 1862.
Coley, Alfred B........................May 11, 1865.
Conrades, August.......................Sept. 24, 1867.
Clancy, John J......................... "   6, 1866.
Cameron, Gideon........................April 2, 1868.
Dwyer, John............................Aug. 21, "
Dreitlein, Henry.......................Sept. 24, 1867.
Davis, D. D ....Oct. 4, 1866.

HONORARY ROLL OF THE

Earl, Edward..........................Dec. 15, 1864.
Eckhardt, Augustus...................June 20, 1867.
Ellison, Thomas (Co. Q. Master, Sergeant.)..Oct. 1, 1862.
Ferris, Harvey L.....................Nov. 6, "
Farrel, William (Publisher, 107 Fulton St.)...Sept. 24, 1868.
Green, Thomas J......................Oct. 4, 1866.
Gegenheimer, John G..................June 15, 1865.
Hutchings, August F..................Oct. 30, 1862.
Heath, Dudley C...................... " "
Head, Benjamin.......................Nov. 16, 1865.
Ireland, A. H........................Oct. 16, 1862.
Jenkins, S. S........................March 6, 1863.
Koch, Frederick......................Sept. 24, 1867.
Kimmerman, A.........................April 3, 1866.
Kutner, David........................Sept. 19, 1867.
Lindsley, Walter I...................April 2, 1868.
Lyall, James.........................May 27, 1858.
Lyon, Allen D........................Jan. 17, 1867.
Myers, Wm. H.........................Oct. 16, 1862.
Mathews, Horace B....................March 30, 1863.
Mayforth, Geo........................Oct. 12, 1865.
Myrack, F. B. (Grad. of Fall R., Mass.) Insti..Sept. 6, 1866.
Mooney, M. I.........................Oct. 17, 1867.
Mullen, James W......................June 11, 1861.
Owens, John..........................Sept. 6, 1866.
O'Brien, Joseph......................Aug. 16, "
Pfaeler, Emile.......................Nov. 16, 1865.
Parris, James........................Sept. 24, 1867.
Rothstein, Lazarus...................June 20, 1868.
Rosenthal, William...................Oct. 4, 1866.
Schea, Richard.......................May 18, 1865.
Seaman, Charles L....................Aug. 16, 1866.
Singers, James A.....................April 25, 1866.
Schmidt, Frederick...................Sept. 24, 1867.
Stevens, Henry N.....................Oct. 3, 1867.
Silberies, Theo. W...................May 22, 1862.
Sudlow, Wm. B. (Graduate of Columbia Col.)..Oct. 1, 1868.
Thomas, Charles, brother of Theodore Thomas,
   the celebrated Orchestra Leader.........May 18, 1865.
Theurner, Chris......................Oct. 30, 1862.
Voss, Louis..........................Sept. 19, 1867.
Weeks, Charles.......................March 21, "
Wassweiler, Chris.................... " 15, 1866.
Weiss, Nicholas......................Oct. 16, 1862.
Wilson, Thomas....................... " 4, 1866.
Young, Alexander..................... " 16, 1862.
Young, Stewart....................... " "

K Company.

This corps takes the place of Company L, transferred from the Twelfth in the beginning of the year 1858.
In 1861, it was commanded by Capt. R. Olmstead and First Lieut. Gardner.
At the bombardment of Maryland Heights, K Company was under the command of Capt. Barclay. At Harper's Ferry, this organization acted in a most gallant manner.
Frederick Stevens, after leaving this company in 1863, went on board the Weehawken, and fought at the battle of Charleston. He subsequently was made a commissioned officer on board the New Ironsides.
George Munger was a corporal in this company at the commencement of the rebellion. After the last campaign of the Twelfth, he removed to St. Louis, and was made Inspector of Military Stores.
William Regan, after having served several years in K Company, enlisted in a regiment raised in Burlington, Vt., went with it to Virginia, fought during the seven days' fight, and though frequently wounded, returned as Major of the regiment, in which he went forth as a private.
Capt. John Fahnestock, at present in command of K Company, is an officer of experience, and thoroughly qualified for the duties of his position.

PRESENT MEMBERS OF K COMPANY.

COMMISSIONED OFFICERS.

Date of Commission.
Captain, John Fahnestock..............Aug. 30, 1867.
First Lieutenant, Robert Donald...........Feb. 15, 1868.
Second Lieutenant, Isaac Whitenack........

DRUMMERS.

Date of Certificate.
Ambrose Horton........................Feb. 7, 1866.
Charles J. McKay......................Oct. 13, 1867.

SERGEANTS.

Date of Warrant.
First Sergeant, James Snodgrass...........Feb. 13, 1868.
Second Sergeant, George W. Heller........ " "
Third Sergeant, Charles W. Henry......... " "
Fourth Sergeant, James H. Cochrane....... " "
Fifth Sergeant, ―― ――..................

CORPORALS.

George Richardson.......................June 6, 1866.
Lindsey Williamson...................... " "
Edward Roe.............................Feb. 13, 1868.
Eugene Limberger....................... " 5, "
Adam Meldrum..........................June 3, "

PRIVATES.

Date of Certificate.
Anderson, James........................July 11, 1866.
Asten, James R.........................Sept. 11, 1867.
Allen, Wm. G..........................Feb. 13, 1868.
Bedell, Richard........................Jan. 6, 1864.
Carter, Joseph........................May 27, 1862.
Champ, James..........................March 30, 1864.
Davies, John W........................June 1, 1868.
Emery, Thomas H.......................May 27, 1862.
Eagan, Thomas I.......................Oct. 7, 1863.
Figel, John...........................March 6, 1867.
Gardner, Joseph W.....................Sept. 11, "
Gardner, William S....................Aug. 1, 1866.

TWELFTH REGIMENT.

Johnson, Andrew.......................April 6, 1864.
Mulry, James B........................Feb. 24,   "
McBride, John.........................April 6,   "
Oberlies, William.....................May 27, 1862.
Parshall, William V...................July 11, 1866.
Powers, Richard T.....................May 27, 1862.
Penrose, John.........................   "   "
Pincus, Newman........................Feb. 24, 1864.
Penrose, William J....................Oct. 7,   "
Pehit, Henry J........................Aug. 6, 1865.
Smith, William........................Jan. 27, 1864.
Wheaton, Jonas S......................April 6,   "

BILL OF DRESS

"INDEPENDENCE GUARD"

TWELFTH INFANTRY,

NATIONAL GUARD, STATE OF NEW YORK,

ADOPTED AT A MEETING OF THE RANK AND FILE, HELD AT THE STATE ARSENAL, CORNER OF THIRTY-FIFTH STREET AND SEVENTH AVENUE, 5TH DECEMBER, 1868, AND BY THE BOARD OF OFFICERS, 8TH JANUARY, 1869.

GENERAL HEADQUARTERS, S. N. Y.
Adjutant General's Office.

ALBANY, *January* 30, 1869.

Special Orders,
No. 7.

The Bill of Dress adopted for the use of the Twelfth Regiment National Guard, at a meeting of the Rank and File, December 5, 1868, and by its Board of Officers, January 8, 1869, and approved by the Brigade and Division Commanders, is hereby allowed and authorized to be worn by said Regiment.

By order of the Commander-in-Chief.

FRANKLIN TOWNSEND,
Adjutant General.

Official,
W. H. MURPHY,
Adjutant Twelfth Infantry.

FULL DRESS UNIFORM.

COAT.—FIELD OFFICERS.

DRESS coat, dark blue cloth, double breasted; with standing collar of same material, to meet and hook under the chin, with two black hooks and eyes, and to be of such height as to permit of the free turning of the chin over it. On each side of the collar, commencing at the end, a loop of seven-line army gold lace, four and one-half inches long, with a small State button on the rear end of each loop. On breast of coat there shall be two rows of State Regulation buttons, seven in each row, placed at equal distances from collar to waist, the distance between the rows to be six inches at the collar (measuring from eye to eye), and three and one-half inches at the waist, diminishing in distance in a straight line from top to bottom. The sleeves cut without cuffs, slash-flaps of white cloth on the sleeves five and one-half inches long, scalloped so as to present three points two and one-half inches long, and two curves two inches wide, four loops of seven-line army gold lace on each flap, at equal distances apart, with a small State button on the outer end of each loop. The top of the skirts to be half the width of the forepart and diminish to two and one-half inches at the bottom. Each back to be one and three-quarter inches at the waist and two and one-half inches at the bottoms; two large State buttons at the hip. The skirts lined with white farmer's satin, and turned up with white cloth on both back and front skirts; the turn-ups on the front to commence at the skirt strap, and on the back two inches below the hip button, the back seam to be closed that distance down. The turn-ups to be one and one quarter inches at the top and widen downward to one inch in width at a place on the skirt two and one-half inches from the bottom, then curve out to a point, and meet at two and one-half inches from the bottom of the skirts, the turn-ups to form a half circle above and below the points, with a large gold-embroidered bugle on the points of the turn-ups. On the centre of each skirt, a flap of white cloth seven inches long, scalloped so as to present three points three inches long, and two curves two inches wide, the upper edge to be two inches below, and ranging with the waist seam; four loops of seven-line army gold lace on each flap at equal distances apart, with a small State button on the outer end of each loop. The skirts to extend to within two inches of the bend of the knee.

COMMISSIONED STAFF OFFICERS.

The same as Field Officers, *except* that there shall be two rows of Regulation Staff buttons on breast of coat, nine in each row, equi-distant.

LINE OFFICERS.

The same as Field Officers, *except* that there shall be two rows of State Regulation buttons on breast of coat, nine in each row, equi-distant.

NON-COMMISSIONED OFFICERS AND PRIVATES.

The same as Field Officers, *except* it shall be single breasted, with three rows of large State buttons, nine in each row, the top button of the outer row to be three and one-half inches from the top one of the centre row (measuring from eye to eye), and the buttons of the outer row to increase in distance from the centre row to the third button from the top, which is to be the greatest across (six and one-half inches), and then diminish with an inward curve to two and one-half inches from the centre row at the waist, and the skirts will only extend to within five inches of the bend of the knee, and instead of being half the width of the forepart shall measure one inch less across the top than the strap, diminishing as above stated, and be lined with black farmer's satin. The slashes on collar, sleeves, and skirts to be white cloth, with four large State buttons on the sleeve and skirt-flaps, and one small State button on the rear end of each collar-flap, and one large State button, instead of bugle, on the bottom of each skirt.

Trowsers.

Light blue. Doeskin for Commissioned Officers; kersey for Non-Commissioned Officers, Musicians, and Privates; cut straight, with a stripe of white cloth one and one-quarter inches wide, the back of which to touch the outside seam. A gold cord, one-eighth of an inch wide each side of the stripe, for Commissioned Officers.

Hat.

All Officers, Non-Commissioned Officers, and men will wear a hat of *felt, covered with mazarine blue cloth*, braided with white worsted braid one-quarter of an inch wide, in shape of a V on both sides of body, and one row of narrow white worsted braid around the top and bottom, with band of patent leather and pressed tip. Height in front four inches, rear seven and three-quarter inches. Black patent-leather chin-strap, five-eighths of an inch wide, with slide and buckle. Vizor of heavy patent leather and bound corners, round, and from one to one and one-half inches wide, lining of black roan leather, chinstrap fastened by regimental buttons.

Commissioned Officers' hats will be braided with gold lace, instead of white worsted.

Hat Ornament.

Commissioned Officers, gold-embroidered bugle, with silver embroidered numeral "12" in centre. Non-Commissioned Officers and men, regimental pattern.

PLUMES.

Field Officers will wear in their hats a white heron plume, mazarine-blue feathers at the base.

All other Commissioned Officers will wear a plume of white cock feathers, with blue top, drooping about six inches in front and three inches behind, brass wire shank and gilt socket.

Commissioned Staff Officers will conform to State Regulations in regard to color.

POMPON.

All enlisted men will wear in their hats a pompon of worsted, white body, with blue top three quarters of an inch deep, the whole three inches long and one and three-quarter inches in diameter at top, tapering to bottom, with brass plume socket.

EPAULETTES.

For Commissioned Officers, as prescribed in the General Regulations, State of New York.

For Enlisted Men, regimental pattern, dark blue cloth, white worsted fringe.

Non-Commissioned Staff Officers, First Sergeants, and Company Quarter-Master Sergeants to have one row of gold fringe, same size as worsted, and intermixed with same.

CHEVRONS FOR NON-COMMISSIONED OFFICERS

To be made of seven-line army gold lace, cushioned upon white cloth, to show an edging of white cloth on each side of the lace, to be worn as directed by General Regulations, State of New York.

Service chevrons of the same material may be worn in the manner prescribed in United States Army Regulations.

Belts and Plates.

For Commissioned Officers as prescribed by the General Regulations, State of New York.

For enlisted men, two cross belts of white webbing two and one-quarter inches wide, and waist belt two inches wide of same material. The cartridge-box belt and bayonet belt crossed on the chest, so as to show but two of the centre row of buttons above the breastplate, and to be fixed with a convex brass plate three and one-quarter inches long and two and one-quarter inches wide, the corners cut off, a raised ornamental German figure 12, two inches long, to be placed in centre of same; a brass pin at back of plate. The waistplate to be of brass, with French fastenings, two and one-half inches wide, corners cut off, with a raised German silver company letter, one and one-quarter inches long, on centre of same.

For Non-Commissioned Staff Officers the same, omitting cartridge-box belt; and to have on waistplates the letters "N. Y.," seven-eighths of an inch long, instead of company letter.

Cartridge-Box and Cap-Pouch.

Regimental patterns.

Bayonet-Scabbard.

Plain black leather, 18 inches, with brass tip at bottom and brass socket at top, extending down within the leather at least one-quarter of an inch, and hook for fastening in frog.

Sashes, Swords, Scabbards, and Knots.

All Commissioned and Non-Commissioned Officers to wear swords, etc., as prescribed in General Regulations, State of New York.

Non-Commissioned Staff Officers having a frog attached to cross belt, and Company Sergeants having a frog attached to waist belt, for carrying the same.

NUMERALS AND LETTERS.

All letters on the uniform shall be of the old English style, and all numerals according to the subjoined pattern 12.

CHASSEUR UNIFORM.

Commissioned Officers as per General Regulations.

NON-COMMISSIONED OFFICERS AND PRIVATES.—CHASSEUR JACKET.

(Paragraph 1381 General Regulations.)

All Non-Commissioned Officers and Privates shall wear a chasseur jacket, single-breasted, of dark-blue indigo and wool-dyed cloth, with a plait behind, with skirt extending seven inches from the top to the hip; with two slashes in the skirt, one over each hip; an opening in the skirt behind; one row of large State buttons on the breast, placed at equal distances apart; two at the waist, on the back; a stand-up collar, to rise no higher than to permit the chin to turn freely over it; to hook in front at the bottom; to slope up and backward at an angle of 30 degrees on each side. The cuff shall be two and one-half inches deep on each seam, and on the inside of the sleeve to the point of an inverted V; with two smaller buttons on the outer seam of the cuff, the lower one inch from the end of the sleeve. The collar and body of the jacket to be edged with a white cord piping, extending on the upper edge of the cuff, representing an inverted V; one pocket on the left inside of the breast, and a small pocket in the seam on the right side; a loop over the left hip two and three-quarter inches long, one and one-half inches wide at the base, and one inch wide at top, with a button and hole at upper end, trimmed to correspond with jacket. The lining of the jacket shall be dark-colored silesia, and the skirt black farmer's satin.

Chasseur Trowsers.

(Paragraph 1401 General Regulations.)

Light indigo-blue kersey, with six plaits at the waist in front and four behind, with an ornamental trimming of white cord around each pocket, extending four inches below the bottom of the pocket; very full hips, and tapering from the knee to the foot.

Fatigue Cap.

Mazarine-blue cloth top, dark-blue cloth band trimmed with white braid, as per regimental pattern.

For Commissioned Officers same as above, except gold-embroidered bugle in front, inclosing regimental number in three-quarters of an inch silver numerals.

Epaulettes.

For Non-Commissioned Officers and Privates, same as full dress.

Commissioned Officers will wear shoulder-straps as prescribed by General Regulations, State of New York.

Leggings.

Russet leather, as per regimental pattern.

Belts and Plates.

Waist belt of patent leather, one and one-half inches wide, to be fastened with waist plate (oval), two and three-quarter inches long by one and five-eighth inches wide, with company letter, five-eighths of an inch high, of white metal, in centre.

Cartridge-Box, Bayonet-Sheath, and Cap-Pouch.

Regimental patterns.

Great Coat.

(Paragraph 1494 General Regulations.)

The great coat for all Non-Commissioned Officers, Musicians, and Privates shall be of sky-blue indigo kersey, extending four inches below the knee; cut off at the waist; single-breasted, with six large State buttons behind, the two lower ones on the fly; one pocket in the plait behind, and one pocket in the inside left breast; cape 18 inches deep; five small buttons in front; the sleeves without cuffs, lined with brown linen, or heavy silesia; the body of the coat lined with twilled red flannel; canvas through breast and collar.

CONTRACT PRICES OF UNIFORM AND EQUIPMENTS.

Dress coat (white trimmings)	$18 00
Blue kersey trowsers	7 50
Chevrons: First Sergeants	6 00
" Co. Quarter-Master Sergeants	6 00
" Sergeants	5 00
" Corporals	4 00
Dress hat (complete)	5 00
White webb belts	1 00
Breast and waist plates	1 15
Cartridge-box, with ornament, (new)	2 00
Bayonet-scabbard, (new)	75
Frog for bayonet-scabbard	25
Cap-pouch	50
Frog for Non-Commissioned Officers' swords,	50
Alteration of cartridge-box	35
Alteration of bayonet-scabbard	25

EXTRACTS

FROM THE

MILITARY CODE

OF THE

STATE OF NEW YORK.

AN ACT *to provide for the enrollment of the Militia, the organization and discipline of the National Guard of the State of New York, and for the public defense.* Passed April 23, 1862, by a two-thirds vote.

The people of the State of New York, represented in Senate and Assembly, do enact as follows:

OF THE PERSONS SUBJECT TO MILITARY DUTY.

§ 1. All able-bodied white male citizens, and *persons of foreign birth* who shall have declared, on oath, their intention to become citizens under and in pursuance of the laws thereof, between the ages of eighteen and forty-five years, residing in this State, and not exempted by the laws of the United States, shall be subject to military duty, excepting:

1. All persons in the army or navy and volunteer force of the United States, and all ministers of the gospel.

2. Persons who have been or hereafter shall be regularly and honorably discharged from the army or navy of the United States, in consequence of the performance of military duty, in pursuance of any law of this State, and such firemen as are now exempted by law.

3. The commissioned officers who shall have served as such in the militia of this State, or in any one of the United States, for the space of seven years; but no officer shall be so exempt unless by his resignation after such term of service duly accepted, or in some other lawful manner he shall have been honorably discharged.

4. Every non-commissioned officer, musician, and private, of every uniform company or troop raised, or hereafter to be raised, who has or shall hereafter uniform himself according to the provisions of any law of this State, and who shall have performed service in such company or troop for the space of seven years from the time of his enrollment therein, shall be exempt from military duty, except in case of war, insurrection, or invasion. (*As amended by chap.* 425 *of* 1863, § 1, *and by chap.* 612 *of* 1865.)

§ 2. If any member of such company or troop, who shall have been regularly uniformed and equipped, shall, upon his removal out of the beat of such company or troop, or upon the disbandment thereof, enlist into any other uniform company or troop, and uniform and equip himself therefor, and serve in the same, whenever the whole time of his service in such companies or troops, computed together, shall amount to seven years, he shall be exempt from military duty in like manner as if he had served for the whole period in the company or troop in which he was first enrolled.

§ 3. Idiots, lunatics, paupers, habitual drunkards, and persons convicted of infamous crimes, shall not be subject to military duty.

OF THE ENROLLMENT OF PERSONS SUBJECT TO MILITARY DUTY.

§ 4. Under the direction and superintendence of the commander-in-chief, all persons liable to military duty within this State, who are not already members of the organized militia thereof, shall, immediately upon the passage of this act, and from time to time thereafter, as the commander-in-chief shall deem necessary, but as often as once in every two years, be enrolled by the captain or commandant of the company district within whose bounds such person shall reside; or if there be no such captain or commandant, then by an officer to be detailed by the commanding officer of the regiment in which such company district is situated, or to be appointed by the commander-in-chief. Such enrollment shall distinctly specify the names and residences of the persons enrolled, and shall also divide the same into two classes, the persons between the ages of eighteen and thirty years to constitute one class, and the persons between the ages of thirty and forty-five years to constitute the other class. Four copies of such enrollment shall be prepared by the officer making the same, one of which, after the same shall have been corrected as hereinafter provided, shall be retained by him, another shall be filed in the office of the town or city clerk in which such company district is situated, if there be such office, another shall be filed in the office of the clerk of the county where such district is situated, and the fourth shall be filed in the adjutant-general's office. The officer making such enrollment may, with the approval of the commander-in-chief, appoint one or more of his non-commissioned officers, or other proper persons, to assist in making said enrollment and copying said rolls. The persons making such enrollment shall be compensated at the rate of one dollar and fifty cents per day for every day necessarily spent in making and copying the same; the number of days to be certified by the commandant of the regiment, and not to exceed ten, and the amount of such compensation to be paid by the comptroller upon production of such certificate, together with the certificates of the town clerk, county clerk, and adjutant-general, that such rolls have been duly filed in their offices. Such rolls shall be so filed on or before the first day of July in each year in which such enrollment shall be made. The officer or person making such enrollment shall, at the time of making the same, serve upon each person enrolled a notice, by delivering the same to him personally, or by leaving it with some person of suitable age and discretion at his place of residence, that he is enrolled as liable to military duty, and that if he claims that he is for any reason exempt from military duty, he must, on or before the fifteenth day of August then next ensuing, file a written statement of such exemption, verified by affidavit, in the office of the town or city clerk, to be designated in said notice. Blank notices for such purpose shall be provided to such enrolling officer by the adjutant-general. (*As amended by chap.* 425 *of* 1863, § 2.)

§ 5. For the purpose of preparing such enrollment, the assessors in each city, village, town, or ward of this State, shall allow captains or commandants of companies, or other officers appointed for that purpose, as above provided, at all proper times to examine their assessment rolls and to take copies thereof; and the clerks of all towns and cities shall in like manner, at all proper times, allow the said commandant or other officer to examine and copy the poll lists on file in their offices.

§ 6. All tavern keepers, keepers of boarding houses, persons having boarders in their families, and any master and mistress of any dwelling house, shall, upon the application of any officer authorized to make such enrollment, give information of the names of all persons residing or lodging in such house, liable to be enrolled, and all other proper information concerning such persons as such officer may demand.

§ 7. If any person of whom information is required by any such officer, in order to enable him to comply with the provisions of this act, shall refuse to give such information, or shall give false information, he shall forfeit and pay ten dollars for each item of information demanded of him by any such officer and falsely stated, and the like sum for each individual name that may be refused, concealed, or falsely stated ; and every person who shall refuse to give his own name and proper information, when applied to by any such officer, or shall give a false name or information, shall forfeit and pay a like sum ; such penalties to be recovered in any court of competent jurisdiction, in the name of the people of the State of New York ; and it is hereby made the duty of such officer to report the names of all persons who may incur any penalty in this section prescribed, to the commandant of the regimental district in which they reside.

§ 8. Whenever an enrollment shall be made, as provided in this act, the county clerk of each county shall cause to be published, once a week, for four weeks previous to the first day of August, in a newspaper published in such county, a notice that such rolls have been completed and filed as aforesaid, which notice shall also specify that any person who claims that he is, for any reason, exempt from military duty, shall, on or before the fifteenth day of August then next ensuing, file a written statement of such exemption, verified by affidavit, in the office of said town or city clerk, or of the county clerk, if there be no such town or city clerk ; and the publication of such notice shall be a sufficient notice of such enrollment of all persons named therein. Such roll shall be made in the form prescribed by the commander-in-chief, and the adjutant-general shall furnish to all commandants of companies suitable blanks and instructions therefor. (*As amended by* § 1, *chap.* 809 *of* 1866.)

§ 9. Such commandant shall not include in said enrollment the names of any officers nor members of the uniformed militia of this State, nor of the officers or members of any fire company ; and the foreman of every fire company in any city, village, or town of this State, shall, before the fifteenth day of May in each year, file in the office of the town or city clerk, a list containing the names of all persons belonging to their respective companies, which list shall show the town or ward in which each member of such company resides.

§ 10. All persons claiming exemptions shall file a written statement of the same, verified by affidavit, in the office of the town or city clerk, or of the county clerk, in case there be no such town or city clerk, on or before the fifteenth day of August, in default of which such person shall lose the benefit of such exemption, except such as are especially exempt by act of congress.

§ 11. The captain, commandant, or other officer making such enrollment, shall thereupon, if such person be exempt, according to law, mark the word "exempt" opposite the name of each person presenting such exemption. If such exemption be permanent, the name of such person shall not be included in any subsequent enrollment. If any person shall swear falsely in such affidavit, he shall be guilty of perjury.

§ 12. The persons thus enrolled shall form the reserve militia of the State of New York; those between the ages of eighteen and thirty years shall constitute the reserve of the first class, and those between the ages of thirty and forty-five years shall constitute the reserve of the second class.

§ 13. The reserve militia of the first and second classes, except such as shall volunteer or be drafted as members of the national guard, as hereinafter provided, shall assemble in their several company districts, armed and equipped as provided by law, for parade and inspection, on the first Monday in September in each year, at such hour and place as the captain or commandant shall designate in orders, to be posted in three public places in said company district for ten days, and shall be under the orders of the captain or commandant of such district; and such captain or commandant shall make a register of all such as shall attend at such parade armed and equipped as aforesaid, to which shall be annexed a list of delinquents, containing the names of all such persons as are on the said enrollment, not marked "exempt" thereon, and who did not attend at such parade, and shall file a copy of the same, on or before the first day of October next following the time of such parade, in the office of the adjutant-general and of the county clerk, and shall also file a list of such delinquents with the board of supervisors and with the county treasurer, on or before the said first day of October. (*As amended by* § 1, *chap.* 809 *of* 1866.)

§·14. All persons duly enrolled, as aforesaid, who shall neglect to attend said parade, shall be subject to a fine of one dollar, which shall be collected by the collector or receiver of taxes of the town or city in which the company district is situated; and the supervisors of the several counties, at their annual meetings, are authorized and directed to annex a list of the several delinquents, with the fines set opposite their respective names, to the assessment rolls of the several towns and wards, and the warrants for the collection of the same shall direct the collectors and receivers of taxes to collect the amount from every person appearing by the said assessment roll liable to pay the same, in the same manner as taxes are collected, the same to be paid to the county treasurer; and when the name of any person between the ages of eighteen and twenty-one years shall appear on the said roll, liable to pay said fine, the said warrant shall direct the collector to collect the same of the father, master, or guardian with whom such person shall reside, or out of any property such minor may have in the city, village, town, or ward, and such collector shall proceed and execute such warrant; and no property now exempt from execution shall be exempt from the payment of such fines. (*As amended by* § 1, *chap.* 809 *of* 1866.)

§ 15. The county treasurer of each county shall, on or before the fifteenth day of March in each year, pay to the comptroller, upon his order, the sum of one dollar for each person named on said list of delinquents; and in case he shall not, on the presentation of such draft, have received all or any of the money directed by this act to be collected and paid to him, he is hereby authorized and directed to borrow an amount sufficient to pay said draft upon the credit of the county, and the sum borrowed shall be a county charge, to be assessed by the board of supervisors of said county, at their next annual meeting, upon the taxable property of said county, and collected as other county assessments shall be assessed and collected ; and it shall be the duty of the county treasurers of the several counties, and the commanding officers of the several regiments, to report and certify under oath to the board of supervisors, at their annual meetings, the deficiencies arising from the non-collection of military fines within their respective counties and regimental districts. (*As amended by* § 1, *chap.* 809 *of* 1866.)

§ 16. The provisions of article first, title three, chapter thirteen, of part first of the Revised Statutes, shall apply to this act so far as the same are applicable.

§ 17. The bond required to be executed by the collector, receiver of taxes, and county treasurer shall apply to any moneys required to be collected for military purposes by this act.

§ 18. Any deficiency arising from the non-collection of said fines shall be a county charge, and shall be raised as aforesaid by the supervisors of said county by taxation on the real and personal estates therein in the manner now provided by law.

§ 19. If any collector or receiver of taxes, county treasurer, town, county, or city clerk, or supervisor, or any other civil or military officer, charged with any duty under the provisions of this act, shall refuse or neglect to perform any of the duties required of him by this act, he shall forfeit and pay the sum of not less than twenty-five nor more than one hundred dollars for each and every offense, to be recovered in the name of the people of the State of New York, and if any of such officers shall willfully neglect or refuse to perform such duties as are hereby required, he shall be deemed guilty of a misdemeanor, and it shall be the duty of the district attorney of any county within which such delinquent offender resides, upon the complaint of the commanding officer of the regiment, to prosecute the same. Any penalty incurred and paid or collected under this section shall be paid into the treasury of the county and belong to the military fund of such regiment.

OF THE GENERAL ORGANIZATION OF THE MILITIA, AND THE ORGANIZATION OF THE NATIONAL GUARD OF THE STATE OF NEW YORK.

Of Organization.

§ 20. The commander-in-chief of the militia of this State shall organize and arrange the same, and the districts therefor, into divisions, brigades, regiments, battalions, squadrons, troops, batteries, and companies, and cause the same to be numbered as nearly in conformity to the laws of the United States as local circumstances and the public convenience may permit, and may alter, divide, annex, or consolidate the same and the districts thereof, and dismiss supernumerary officers, who were made such by an excess of officers of equal grade being thrown into any division, brigade, regimental, or company district. The present divisions, brigades, regiments, battalions, troops, squadrons, batteries, and companies, and the districts thereof, shall remain as now established by law, subject to the power of the commander-in-chief, to alter, divide, annex, or consolidate the same as above set forth. Regimental districts, except in cities, shall conform, as nearly as convenient, to the assembly districts of this State.

§ 21. The organized militia of the State shall be known as the "National Guard of the State of New York," and shall consist of eight divisions, and such number of brigades, regiments, companies, and battalions and such batteries, troops, or squadrons, as the commander-in-chief shall determine and designate. Provided, that the aggregate organized force of the national guard, in time of peace, to be fully armed, equipped, and uniformed, shall not exceed the number of fifty thousand non-commissioned officers and privates; but the commander-in-chief shall have power in cases of war or insurrection, or imminent danger thereof, to make further drafts of the militia, and to form new regiments, battalions, batteries, and troops, and to organize the same, as the exigencies of the service shall require. (*As amended by* § 1, *chap.* 809 *of* 1866.)

§ 22. The national guard shall include the present uniformed militia of this State, and such volunteers as shall enroll themselves therein in the several districts of this State, and such persons as may be drafted therein, as hereinafter provided, and shall be organized, and shall serve as engineers, artillery, light artillery, cavalry, infantry, and rifles, as the commander-in-chief shall direct.

§ 23. The commander-in-chief is hereby authorized and empowered, so soon as may be convenient after the passage of this act, to appoint and commission the brigade, regimental, and company officers, in the first instance, necessary to complete the organization of all military districts hereafter to be created, and to fill all vacancies necessary for the complete organization of all military districts now created in this State, but not sufficiently organized for an election. All officers superseded by such appointment shall become supernumerary officers.

§ 24. The commandant of each regimental district, for the purpose of organization, is hereby authorized and required to appoint the non-commissioned officers required by law for each company in his district, and to issue to such non-commissioned officers the proper warrants of their appointment, until the organization of such regiment shall be complete.

§ 25. The organization of the national guard shall conform to the provisions of the laws of the United States, and their system of discipline and exercise shall conform as nearly as may be to that of the army of the

United States, as it now is, or may hereafter be prescribed by congress.

§ 26. Company officers shall use their best efforts to obtain sufficient volunteers to raise their respective companies to the number of, at least, sixty-four non-commissioned officers and privates, which number is hereby .fixed as the minimum, and one hundred as the maximum of such company organization. (*As amended by* § 1, *chap.* 809 *of* 1866.)

§ 27. In case of any company of the national guard shall not, on or before the first day of October next, by voluntary enlistments, reach the number of sixty-four privates, or in case such company shall at any time fall below such number, or in case a sufficient number of persons shall not volunteer to organize new companies in the unorganized company districts, it shall be lawful for the commander-in-chief to order a sufficient number of persons, and also fifty per cent. in addition, to be drafted from the reserve militia of the first class, in the manner hereinafter provided, to raise such companies to, and maintain the same at, such number. The persons so drafted shall thereupon be enrolled as members of said company, and, unless they shall furnish substitutes, as hereinafter provided, shall be subject to the duties herein mentioned, and in case of non-performance of such duties, shall be subject to the pains and penalties herein mentioned ; and such persons, or their substitutes, shall be entitled to all the privileges and exemptions conferred under any of the terms of this act. (*As amended by chap.* 612 *of the Laws of* 1865.)

§ 28. To every company there shall be one captain, one first, one second lieutenant, four sergeants, four corporals, and three musicians, except in companies of artillery and cavalry, which may have one first and two second lieutenants, provided, however, that whenever any company shall exceed fifty rank and file, it may have five sergeants and eight corporals.

§ 29. Companies shall be formed in separate company districts when practicable, but the commander-in-chief may, in his discretion, organize more companies than one in the same district, or parts of a company in different districts.

§ 30. Each division shall consist of not less than two brigades, each brigade not less than two regiments, each regiment not less than eight battalion companies of sixty-four non-commissioned officers and privates. Whenever any company shall fall below the number of sixty-four non-commissioned officers and privates, such company may be consolidated or disbanded; and whenever any regimental organization shall fall below the number of eight battalion companies, or an aggregate force of five hundred and twelve non-commissioned officers and privates, such regiment shall thereupon be designated as a battalion, but shall retain its regimental number, unless such battalion shall be consolidated or disbanded. (*As amended by* § 1, *chap.* 809 *of* 1866.)

§ 31. The commander-in-chief shall have power to organize, under the provisions of this act, battalions of infantry and rifles, and battalions, batteries, or companies of artillery, or for special services where it is not expedient or convenient to form regimental organizations, or whenever the exigencies of the service may require.

§ 32. No non-commissioned officer, musician, or private belonging to any troop of cavalry or company of artillery, light artillery, riflemen, or infantry, shall leave the troop or company to which he belongs to serve as a fireman in any fire company now raised or hereafter to be raised in any city or county; nor shall he leave such troop or company and enlist in any other, without the written consent of the commandant of the regiment, battalion, or battery, and of the squadron, troop, or company to which he belongs, except he shall have removed out of the beat of such troop or company. Such exception shall not apply to any troop or company situate in any of the cities of this State.

§ 33. No person under the age of twenty-one years shall hereafter enlist in or join any uniform troop or company, without the consent of his parent or guardian, master or mistress, unless drafted in accordance with the provisions of this act.

§ 34. Every officer of the line and staff, and every officer and private of any uniform company of this State, shall provide himself, according to the provisions of this act, with a uniform complete, which shall be such as the commander-in-chief shall prescribe, and subject to such restrictions, limitations, and alterations as he may order.

§ 35. Any non-commissioned officer or private may, upon his enlistment, or upon being drafted, in accordance with the provisions of this act, if he so select, be furnished at the expense of the State with proper uniform and equipments of his regiment or corps; in such case an entry to that effect shall be made on the company roll, and such uniform shall be furnished by the quartermaster-general's department upon the requisition of the commandant of the regiment or battalion; but such uniform and equipments shall in no case be different from those prescribed by the general regulations of the military forces of the State of New York, unless by special authority of the commander-in-chief, and only two uniforms shall be furnished by the State to any non-commissioned officer or private during his term of enlistment, except in case of actual service in garrison or field duty. (*As amended by* § 1, *chap.* 809 *of* 1866.)

§ 36. In case such uniform and equipments be furnished in accordance with the last preceding section; the same shall be left at the company armory for safe keeping, and the person applying for the same shall be charged with the value thereof, and shall be entitled to receive half pay only for services under this act, at drills, parades, encampments, and lake and sea-coast defense duty, until the sum charged against him therefor shall have been liquidated by such service, when such uniform and equipment shall become the property of such person.

§ 37. Whoever shall secrete, sell, dispose of, offer for sale, or in any manner pawn or pledge any uniform or equipments, the property of the people of this State, and any member of or substitute in the national guard who shall, when not on duty, wear any such uniform or equipments without the permission of his commanding officer, shall be deemed guilty of a misdemeanor, and shall be punished by imprisonment in the county jail for not less than one nor more than two months, or by a fine of not more than one hundred nor less than fifty dollars. (*As amended by* § 1, *chap.* 809 *of* 1866.)

§ 38. The quartermaster-general shall, under the direction and with the approval of the commander-in-chief, cause to be manufactured the uniforms and equipments which may, from time to time, be required for each regiment, for the purposes mentioned in this act. And the comptroller, upon the order of the commander-in-chief, shall draw his warrant upon the treasurer for such sums as shall, from time to time, be expended for the purchase or manufacture of said uniforms and equipments; provided, always, that the price paid for the same shall in no case exceed the prices paid for uniforms and equipments of like quality for the army of the United States. (*As amended by chap.* 612 *of* 1865.)

§ 39. All vouchers and accounts under the last preceding section shall, from time to time, be audited by a committee, to consist of the comptroller, treasurer, and secretary of State.

§ 40. The commander-in chief shall, from time to time, direct such books, as to him shall appear expedient, as a guide for the military forces of this State, to be provided, and shall furnish the same to all commissioned officers at the expense of the State.

§ 41. The commander-in-chief shall cause each company, squadron, troop, battery, battalion, regiment, brigade, and division to be numbered or lettered in such manner as he shall deem proper and best calculated to secure uniformity. Each company, squadron, troop, battery, battalion, regiment, brigade, and division shall be known by its number and designation, which shall be registered at the adjutant-general's office.

§ 42. Non-commissioned officers shall be chosen from

the members of the company to which they belong. All commissioned officers residing in any city or incorporated village in this State shall be deemed to be within the bounds of their respective commands, providing any part of the military district to which they properly belong shall be located within such city or village.

§ 43. All existing uniformed companies, in any such regimental district, city, or village, shall be deemed to be organized under the provisions of this act; but no such company shall be so constituted, unless at the time of such application it contains thirty-two non-commissioned officers and privates.

§ 44. Whenever six uniformed companies shall be organized in any of the regimental districts of this State, the commander-in-chief shall order an election to be held for the choice of suitable persons to fill the offices of colonel, lieutenant-colonel, and major in such regiment, by directing some suitable officer to give the proper notice of such election, and to preside thereat, unless such officer shall already have been elected or appointed; but the colonel so elected or appointed shall not be commissioned until eight battalion companies of sixty-four non-commissioned officers and privates shall be fully organized. (*As amended by* § 1, *chap*. 809 *of* 1860.)

§ 45. As soon as the field officers in the regiments in any of the brigade districts of this State shall be duly chosen and commissioned, the commander-in-chief shall order an election to be held for the choice of a suitable person to fill the office of brigadier-general and brigade inspector in such brigade district, by directing some suitable officer to give the pro-notices of such election and preside thereat, unless such brigadier-general and brigade inspector shall already have been elected or appointed, as provided by this act.

§ 46. All commissioned officers rendered supernumerary by the provisions of this act, and every officer rendered supernumerary by any consolidation or alteration of regiments, battalions, squadrons, troops, or companies, shall be entitled to all the privileges conferred by any preceding law (except command), and shall be exempt from the performance of any military duty, except in cases of war and insurrection, provided they shall, within one year after being so rendered supernumerary, have reported themselves to the adjutant-general as such ; provided, however, that no officer rendered supernumerary shall be entitled to vote at any election held for the choice of officers, or serve as a member of any court-martial.

§ 47. Volunteers under the provisions of this act may be received in any company of the national guard, whether such volunteer reside in the company district or not ; but persons liable to military duty shall be drafted only in the district where they may reside.

§ 48. Any officer, non-commissioned officer, musician, or uniformed private who may change his residence from within the bounds of the first division into any adjacent county, or from within any county adjacent into the said division district, shall not thereby vacate his office or post, but he shall be held to duty in the division, brigade, regiment, troop, or company to which he was attached at the time of such change of residence, and shall be eligible to promotion, election, or appointment to office therein, and he shall be subject to duty therein, and shall be entitled to all privileges, immunities, and exemptions allowed by law, and shall be liable to fines and penalties, and the collection of them, in the same manner as if such change of residence had not taken place, and process for the collection of such fines and penalties may be executed in either New York or any adjacent county. (*As amended by* § 1, *chap.* 809 *of* 1866.)

ON THE ELECTION AND APPOINTMENT OF MILITARY OFFICERS AND THE TENURE OF THEIR OFFICES.

§ 49. All major-generals, and the commissary-general, shall be nominated by the governor, and appointed by him, with the consent of the senate.

§ 50. The resolution of the senate, concurring in any

nomination made by the governor to a military office, shall be certified by the president and clerk of the senate, and be transmitted to the adjutant-general, who shall issue the commission and record the same in books to be provided by him.

§ 51. The staff of the commander-in-chief shall consist of the adjutant-general, an inspector-general, engineer-in-chief, judge-advocate-general, quartermaster-general, commissary-general of subsistence, paymaster-general, surgeon-general, and three aids, who shall be appointed by the governor, and whose commission shall expire with the time for which the governor shall have been elected.

§ 52. The commissary-general shall hereafter be known as the commissary-general of ordnance, and shall not enter on the duties of his office until he shall have taken the oath of office prescribed in the constitution. Such oath shall be taken before any officer authorized to administer the same oath to the attorney-general within the same period, and subject to the same regulations.

§ 53. Captains, subalterns, and non-commissioned officers of organized regiments, shall be chosen by the written or printed votes of the members of their respective companies; field officers of organized regiments and battalions, by the written or printed votes of the commissioned officers of their respective regiments and battalions; and brigadier-generals and brigade inspectors, by the written or printed votes of the field officers of their respective brigades, if organized.

§ 54. Major-generals, brigadier-generals, and commanding officers of regiments or battalions, shall appoint the staff officers of their respective divisions, brigades, regiments, or battalions, whose term of office shall expire when the persons appointing them shall retire from office; but they shall continue to hold such office until their successor shall be appointed and have qualified.

§ 55. The commissioned officers of the national guard shall be commissioned by the governor, but he may, in his discretion, withhold such commission in order to determine the qualifications of the person for the office to which he shall have been elected or appointed; and in case of a general or field officer, if upon reference to the inspector-general or an examining board, and in case of a line officer, upon reference to his brigade commander, such person shall be adjudged unqualified for such office, another officer shall, within ten days after due notice of such adverse decision, be elected or appointed, and in default of such election, the vacancy shall be filled by the commander-in-chief, and no commissioned officer can be removed from office unless by the senate, on recommendation of the governor, stating the grounds on which such removal is recommended, or by the decision of a court-martial, or retiring or examining board, or pursuant to law. But whenever any regiment shall fall below the minimum strength, as is established by this act, and the same shall have been designated as a battalion, the colonel shall be relieved from command of such battalion, and rendered supernumerary, by order of the commander-in-chief. (*As amended by chap.* 612 *of* 1865, *and by* § 1, *chap.* 809 *of* 1866.)

§ 56. Sergeant-majors, quartermaster-sergeants, sergeant standard-bearers, and drum-majors shall be appointed by the commanding officer of the regiment or battalion to which they shall belong, by warrant under the hand of such commanding officer, and shall hold their offices during his pleasure.

§ 57. Whenever the office of a brigadier-general is vacant in any organized brigade, the commander-in-chief shall issue an order for an election to fill the vacancy, and shall designate a major-general or some other proper officer to preside at such election.

§ 58. The officer so designated shall cause a written or printed notice to be served on each of the field officers of the brigade in which the vacancy exists, at least ten days previous to the election, specifying the time and place of holding such election.

§ 59. Whenever the office of any field officer in any organized regiment or battalion is vacant, the commanding officer of the brigade to which such regiment or battalion belongs, shall cause a written or printed notice to be served on each commissioned officer in such regiment or battalion, of an election to fill the vacancy. The notice shall specify the time and place of holding the election, and be served at least five days before such election shall take place.

§ 60. Whenever the office of a captain or subaltern in any organized company or troop is vacant, the commanding officer of the regiment or battalion to which such company or troop belongs shall cause a written or printed notice of an election to fill the vacancy, to be served on the members of such company or troop, at least three days before the election shall take place, and shall specify in such notice the time and place of the election.

§ 61. All notices for any election shall be served on the persons entitled to vote thereat, in the same manner as non-commissioned officers, musicians, and privates are warned to attend a parade, as prescribed in section one hundred and thirty-nine of this act.

§ 62. The officer issuing the notice shall designate some proper person or persons to serve the same or to direct such service; and the person so designated shall make a return of the persons notified, and of the manner of the services.

§ 63. The return, if made by a commissioned officer, shall be authenticated by his certificate on honor; if by a non-commissioned officer, by the oath of the person making such service. The oath may be administered by any magistrate, or by the officer issuing the notice.

§ 64. The officer causing the notice to be given for any of the aforesaid elections, shall attend at the time and place of holding such elections; he shall organize the meeting and preside thereat, and may, for sufficient cause, adjourn the same from time to time.

§ 65. If the officer causing the notices to be given shall not attend the meeting for the election, then the officer of the highest rank present, or in case of an equality of rank between two or more, then such of them as the majority of the electors present shall choose, shall preside at such meeting. And the officer issuing such notices shall cause the proper evidence of service of such notices on all the electors to be delivered to such presiding officer. And at meetings for the election of company officers, the company roll, carefully revised, shall in like manner be delivered with such evidence. And if it shall happen at any election for commissioned officers that legal notice has not been given to all the persons entitled to vote thereat, the presiding officer shall adjourn the meeting, and cause such notice to be given. The presence of a person entitled to vote at any election shall be deemed a waiver of his right to take exception to the want of legal notice.

§ 66. The presiding officer at any election for commissioned officers shall keep the polls open at least one hour after the time appointed for holding the same. He shall then publicly canvass the votes received from the electors for the officers to be elected, and shall forthwith declare the result, and give notice to every person elected of his election. If such person shall not, within ten days after being notified of his election, signify to such officer his acceptance, he shall be considered as declining the office to which he shall have been chosen, and an election shall be held for a new choice.

§ 67. Immediately after the person elected shall have signified his acceptance, the officer who shall have presided at the election shall, in case of the election of a brigadier-general, communicate the same to the commander-in-chief; and in all other cases, if not himself the commanding officer of the brigade, shall certify to such commanding officer the names of the persons duly elected.

§ 68. If at any election an officer, then in commission, shall be elected to fill a vacancy, and shall accept, the electors present, whether such officer be present or absent, shall proceed to elect a person to fill the place of the officer so promoted, if the officers or persons assembled at such meeting have authority to make the choice.

§ 69. The commanding officers of brigades shall transmit the names of persons duly elected and approved, or appointed to offices in their respective brigades, to the commander-in-chief, to the end that commissions may be issued to them.

§ 70. Every person thinking himself aggrieved by the proceedings at any election for a commissioned officer may appeal, if the election be for a brigadier-general, to the commander-in-chief, and in other cases to the commanding officer of the brigade to which such person belongs.

§ 71. The officer appealed to shall have power to administer oaths, and shall hear and determine the appeal; and if in his opinion the proceedings at such election are illegal, he shall declare the election void, and shall order an election to be held without delay for a new choice.

§ 72. Any person concerned may appeal from the decision of the commanding officer of the brigade to the commander-in-chief, who shall hear and determine such appeal, and, in case it shall be necessary, order a new election.

§ 73. The commander-in-chief may make such rules and regulations relative to appeals as he shall deem necessary and proper to give full effect to the provisions of the constitution and of this act.

§ 74. The commander-in-chief shall issue commissions to all officers duly elected or appointed in pursuance of the provisions of this act; and every officer duly commissioned shall, within ten days after his commission shall be tendered to him, or within ten days after he shall be personally notified that the same is held in readiness for him, by any superior officer, take and subscribe the oath prescribed in the constitution of this State; and in case of neglect or refusal to take such oath within the time mentioned, he shall be deemed to have resigned said office, and a new election shall be forthwith ordered to fill his place. The neglect or refusal of an officer elect to take such oath shall be no excuse for neglect of duty until another shall be duly commissioned in his place.

§ 75. Every commissioned officer shall take and subscribe such oath before a judge or some court of record in this State, county clerk, commissioner to take affidavits, justice of the peace, or some general or field officer who has previously taken it himself, and who is hereby authorized to administer the same.

§ 76. A certificate of the oath shall be indorsed by the officer administering the same on the commission, and a copy thereof shall be filed in the adjutant-general's office.

§ 77. No fee shall be received for administering any such oath; or indorsing such certificate.

§ 78. Any organized company or troop may, at any meeting thereof, elect non-commissioned officers to fill any vacancy therein.

§ 79. Such election shall be directed and conducted by the commanding officer of such company or troop for the time being, who shall certify the names of the persons elected to the commanding officer of the regiment or battalion to which the company or troop belongs, who shall decide upon the legality of the election, and shall issue warrants to the persons duly elected.

§ 80. The commandants of companies or troops may, whenever they deem it necessary, call a special meeting of their respective companies or troops for an election of non-commissioned officers.

§ 81. A majority of the votes of all persons present at an election of brigadier-general shall be necessary to a choice ; in all other cases a plurality shall be sufficient.

§ 82. No officer shall be considered out of the service on the tender of his resignation until it shall have been accepted by the commander-in-chief. The commanding officers of brigades shall receive the resignations of such commissioned officers as may resign in their respective brigades, and shall transmit the same to the adjutant-general. Resignations of all other commissioned officers shall be made direct to the commander-in-chief.

§ 83. No officer shall be permitted to resign his commission who shall be under arrest, or shall be returned to a court-martial for any deficiency or delinquency; and no resignation shall be accepted unless the officer tendering the same shall furnish to the adjutant-general satisfactory evidence that he has delivered all moneys in his hands as such officer, and all books and other property of the State in his possession, to his next superior or inferior officer, or to the officer authorized by law to receive the same, and that his accounts for money or public property are correct.

§ 84. In time of war, or when the military forces of this State are in actual service, resignations shall take effect thirty days from the date of the order of acceptance, unless otherwise specially ordered by the commander-in-chief.

§ 85. On accepting the resignation of any officer, the commander-in-chief shall cause the necessary notices and orders to be given for an election to fill the vacancy so created; provided, however, that when the military forces of this State shall be in the actual service thereof, or in the service of the United States in time of war, insurrection, invasion, or imminent danger thereof, the commander-in-chief shall fill all vacancies of commissioned officers by appointment.

§ 86. Every officer who shall move out of the bounds of his command (unless such removal shall not be beyond the bounds of a city in which such command shall lie in whole or in part), and every officer who shall be absent from his command twelve months without leave of the commanding officer of his brigade, shall be considered as having vacated his office, and a new election shall be held, without delay, to fill the vacancy so created, except as above provided.

§ 87. No person shall be allowed to vote at any election for a commissioned or non-commissioned officer of a company, unless he is an actual member of such company where he shall offer to vote, and liable to do military duty therein.

§ 88. If any person offering to vote at any election for a commissioned officer of a company, shall be challenged as unqualified by any person entitled to vote thereat, the presiding officer shall declare to the person so challenged the qualifications of an elector.

§ 89. If he shall state himself to be duly qualified, and the challenge shall not be withdrawn, the presiding officer shall then tender him the following oath :

"You do swear (or affirm) that you are an actual member of the company commanded by   , and that you are liable to do military duty therein."

§ 90. The commissioned officer who shall receive a commission for any subordinate officer, shall, within thirty days thereafter, give notice thereof to the person entitled to it.

§ 91. The commander-in-chief is hereby authorized, so often as he may deem that the good of the service requires, to appoint a military board or commission of not less than three nor more than five officers, to sit at such place as he shall direct, whose duty it shall be to examine into the physical ability, moral character, capacity, attainments, general fitness for the service, and efficiency of such commissioned officers, as the commander-in-chief may order to be examined by said board, or who may be reported for examination to the adjutant-general by colonels of their regiments, or general officers commanding their brigades or divisions, and upon such report may be ordered to be examined by the commander-in-chief. If the decision of said board be unfavorable to such officer, and be approved by the commander-in-chief, the commission of such officer shall be vacated ; provided, always, that no officer shall be eligible to sit on such board or commission whose rank or promotion would in any way be affected by its proceedings ; and two members, at least, if practicable, shall be of equal rank with the officer to be examined. The officers constituting such board shall receive the same pay and allowances for traveling expenses as members of courts-martial.

§ 92. No officer, whose commission shall have been vacated under the next preceding section, shall be eligible for election to any military office for the period of one year, and his election shall be void; and in case the vacancy so created shall not within thirty days be filled by the election of some other and proper person, the commander-in-chief shall have power to fill such vacancy by appointment.

§ 93. If any commissioned officer shall have become or shall hereafter become incapable of performing the duties of his office, and any commissioned officer who shall have served in the same grade for the continuous period of ten years, may be placed on the supernumerary list and withdrawn from active service and command. (*As amended by* §1, *chap.* 809 *of* 1866.)

§ 94. In order to carry out the provisions of this act, the commander-in-chief shall cause to assemble a board of not less than three nor more than five commissioned officers, all of whom shall have served in the volunteer service of the United States, one of whom at least shall be of the medical staff, to determine the facts as to the nature and occasion of the disability of such officers as appear disabled or unfit, from any cause, to perform military service, such board being hereby invested with the powers of a court of inquiry and court-martial, and their decision shall be subject to like revision as that of such courts by the commander-in-chief. The board, whenever it finds an officer incapacitated for active service, shall report such fact to the commander-in-chief, and if he approves such judgment the disabled officer shall thereupon be placed upon the supernumerary list, according to the provisions of this act; provided, always, that the members of the board shall in every case be sworn to an honest and impartial performance of their duties, and that no officer shall be placed upon the supernumerary list by the action of said board without having had a fair and full hearing before the board, if upon due summons he shall demand it. Provided, that it shall not be necessary to refer any case for the action of such board arising under section ninety-three, except the officers designated by the commander-in-chief to be retired, shall within twenty days after notice that he will be retired, by notice in writing to be served on the adjutant-general, demand a hearing and examination before such board. (*As amended by chap.* 612 *of* 1865, *and by* § 1, *chap.* 809 *of* 1866.)

§ 95. In time of war, insurrection, invasion, or imminent danger thereof, when the military forces of this State shall be in the actual service thereof, the commander-in-chief shall have power, whenever the public interests may in his opinion so require, to suspend from active service such officer or officers as he shall deem it discreet so to suspend, and fill the vacancy thus created by appointment; but no such suspension shall continue for a longer period than thirty days, unless a court-martial shall have in the mean time been ordered for the trial of such officer or officers.

OF THE ORGANIZATION OF THE STAFF DEPARTMENTS.

§ 96. The commander-in-chief shall be entitled to three aids and one military secretary, each with the rank of colonel, and a military messenger with rank of second lieutenant. The commissary-general shall be a member of the staff of the commander-in-chief, and be subject to the provisions of this act. (*As amended by chap.* 612 *of* 1865.)

§ 97. Each major-general shall be entitled to two aids with the rank of major; and each brigadier-general to one aid, with the rank of captain.

§ 98. The adjutant-general shall have the rank of brigadier-general; and in his department there shall be an assistant adjutant-general, with the rank of colonel, and such acting assistants as may be approved by the commander-in-chief; to each division, a division inspector with the rank of colonel; to each brigade, a brigade inspector, to serve also as a brigade major, with the rank of major; and to each regiment or battalion, an adjutant, with the rank of first lieutenant. (*As amended by chap. 612 of 1865.*)

§ 99. The inspector-general shall have the rank of brigadier-general, and his duty shall be to attend to the organization of the militia of this State. He shall inspect every branch connected with the military service, attend the military parades and encampments, when other official duties will permit, and report annually to the commander-in-chief. In the inspector-general's department there shall be an assistant inspector-general, with the rank of colonel, who shall also act, under the directions of the inspector-general, as inspector of military accounts.

§ 100. The engineer-in-chief shall have the rank of brigadier-general ; and there shall be in his department, to each division, a division engineer, with the rank of colonel ; to each brigade, a brigade engineer, with the rank of major ; to each regiment, one engineer, with the rank of captain.

§ 101. In the quartermaster-general's department there shall be a quartermaster-general, with the rank of brigadier-general ; an assistant quartermaster-general, with the rank of colonel ; to each division, a division quartermaster, with the rank of lieutenant-colonel ; to each brigade, a brigade quartermaster, with the rank of captain ; and to each regiment or battalion, a quartermaster, with the rank of lieutenant ; and the quartermaster-general may, with the approval of the commander-in-chief, appoint so many storekeepers as the exigencies of the service may require, not exceeding one to each storehouse. (*As amended by chap.* 334 *of* 1864.)

§ 102. In the department of the commissary-general of subsistence, there shall be a commissary-general of subsistence, with the rank of colonel ; and in his department there shall be so many assistant commissaries, with the rank of captain. as the exigencies of the service may require ; such assistant commissaries to be appointed by the commander-in-chief, and to hold their offices during his pleasure.

§ 103. In the paymaster-general's department there shall be a paymaster-general, with the rank of brigadier-general ; and in his department there shall be an assistant paymaster-general, to be appointed by the paymaster-general, with the rank of colonel ; to each division, a division paymaster, with the rank of major ; and to each brigade, a brigade paymaster, with the rank of captain ; but such paymasters may at any time be detached from service in said brigades or divisions, as well as other officers of the general staff, by order of the commander-in-chief. (*As amended by chap.* 612 *of* 1865.)

§ 104. The commissary-general shall hereafter be known as the commissary-general of ordnance, and shall have the rank of brigadier-general ; and in his department there shall be an assistant, with the rank of colonel ; and so many military storekeepers, for the safe keeping and the preservation of the State arsenals, magazines, fortifications, and military stores belonging to this State, as he may find it necessary to appoint, not exceeding one to each arsenal.

§ 105. In the hospital department there shall be a surgeon-general, with the rank of brigadier-general ; to each division, a hospital surgeon, with the rank of colonel ; to each brigade, a hospital surgeon, with the rank of major ; to each regiment, a surgeon, with the rank of major ; and to each regiment or separate battalion, an assistant surgeon, with the rank of first lieutenant, who shall be commissioned, on the recommendation of the surgeon-general ; but the rank of these officers shall not entitle them to promotion in the line, nor regulate their pay and allowances in the service ; all such officers to be graduates of some incorporated school of medicine. (*As amended by chap.* 612 *of* 1865.)

§ 106. To each regiment or battalion there shall be appointed one chaplain, who shall be a regular ordained minister of a christian denomination.

§ 107. In the judge-advocate's department there shall be a judge-advocate-general, with the rank of brigadier-general ; to each division, a division judge-advocate.

with the rank of colonel; and to each brigade, brigade judge-advocate, with the rank of major.

§ 108. There shall be to each regiment or battalion two sergeant standard-bearers. one sergeant-major, one quartermaster sergeant, one commissary-sergeant, and one drum-major; and to each regiment or battalion of light artillery and cavalry, one trumpet-major.

§ 109. The chief of each staff department shall, under the direction of the commander-in-chief, have command over all subordinate officers in his department, and shall, from time to time, issue orders and instructions for their government and practice.

§ 110. The commander-in-chief is hereby authorized and empowered to organize, in his discretion, the various staff departments, and to prescribe, by rules and regulations, the duties to be performed by the officers connected therewith, which shall, as far as may be, conform to those which are prescribed for the government of the staff department in the army of the United States; and, in time of war, insurrection, or invasion, or imminent danger thereof, and when the exigencies of the service shall require, he may appoint and commission three additional aids upon his staff, with the rank of colonel; and also such number of assistants in the several staff departments, with the rank of lieutenant-colonel or major, as in his judgment shall be necessary. Such assistants shall be selected from persons who have served meritoriously in the volunteer service of the United States, and shall hold their commissions only during the term of service of the staff officer in whose department they shall be appointed, or during the pleasure of the commander-in-chief. (*As amended by chap.* 612 *of* 1865.)

§ 111. Each chief of such department shall prepare and transmit, at the expense of this State, all blank forms of returns, precepts, warrants, and proceedings necessary in his department.

OF THE ORGANIZATION OF BANDS OF MUSICIANS.

§ 112. The commanding officer of each regiment, or

battalion may, in his discretion, organize a band of musicians, and by warrant, under his hand, may appoint a leader of such band.

§ 113. Such musicians shall be subject to the orders of such leader, and be under the command of the commanding officer of the regiment or battalion; and the whole or any part of said band may be required by such commanding officer to appear at any meeting of the officers for military purposes, and at the review and inspection or encampment of such regiment or battalion.

§ 114. The leader of each band shall, whenever required by such commanding officer, make returns to him of the warning of the members of his band, and of the delinquents and delinquencies therein, which returns shall be duly authenticated by the oath of such leader, taken before a field officer of such regiment or battalion.

§ 115. Such return, so sworn to, shall be received as evidence in all cases, in the same manner as like returns of non-commissioned officers of infantry companies.

§ 116. Such commanding officer shall make the like returns of all such delinquents and delinquencies, as in cases of non-commissioned officers and musicians in companies of infantry, and with like effect, and the courts-martial shall impose the like penalties on such delinquent members of said band.

§ 117. The commanding officer of such regiment or battalion shall have authority to disband such band, whether now or hereafter established, and to revoke the warrant of its leader.

§ 118. The provisions of this article shall apply to all musicians employed to serve with the military forces of this State.

OF THE ISSUING AND SAFE KEEPING OF ARMS.

§ 119. Whenever any company, organized under the provisions of this act, shall have reached the minimum number of thirty-two non-commissioned officers and privates, the supervisors of the county in which such company district is situated may, at their discretion, upon the demand of the captain or commandant of such company, countersigned by the colonel of the regiment, together with the certificate of the adjutant general that such company comprises thirty-two non-commissioned officers and privates, who, as appears by the certificate of the colonel of the regiment to which such company is attached, regularly attend the drills and parades of said company, and have been furnished with arms, erect or rent within the bounds of such regiment, for said company, a suitable and convenient armory, drill-room, and place of deposit for the safe keeping of such arms, uniforms, equipments, accoutrements, and camp equipage as shall be furnished such company under the provisions of this act, except in such places where a public armory shall then exist, the same armory to be used by several companies, or shall provide a regimental or battalion armory to be used by all the companies, as the inspector-general and the board of supervisors of the county shall deem expedient. (*As amended by* § 3, *chap.* 4 5 *of* 1863.)

§ 120. The expense of erecting or renting such armories shall be a portion of the county charges of such county, and shall be levied and raised in the same manner as other county charges are levied and paid.

§ 121. In case such armory shall not be erected or rented by the supervisors for the use of such company, the commandant of the regiment, in his discretion, with the approval of the inspector-general, may rent a room or building to be used for the purpose of such armory, and the amount of rent thereof, provided the same shall not exceed the sum of two hundred and fifty dollars for each company, in the several cities of this State, and fifty dollars for companies not located in cities shall be a county charge, and shall be paid by such supervisors, and levied and raised as hereinbefore provided.

§ 122. Such armory, when erected or rented, shall be under the control and charge of the commanding officer of the regiment in whose bounds or district it shall be located; and such commanding officer shall deposit therein all arms and equipments received from time to time for the use of any company in his regiment.

§ 123. The commissary-general of the State shall furnish, on the order of the commander-in-chief, all necessary arms and equipments, suited to the particular company or corps belonging to each regiment, required for camp and field duty; the same to be furnished at the expense of the State, including transportation. But no arms or equipments shall be furnished to any company or corps, unless such company or corps shall be connected with the regular military organization of the State.

§ 124. The commanding officer of each regiment or company shall be responsible for the safe keeping and return of all arms and equipments committed to his charge, and shall execute such bonds as the commander-in-chief shall require from time to time; and no company shall be so furnished until bonds for the safe keeping and return shall be made out and approved by the commander-in-chief, and until a suitable armory or place of deposit shall be assigned, rented, or erected, in such regiment.

§ 125. The commanding officer of any regiment or company who shall have received, according to the provisions of this act, any arms and equipments from the State for the use of his regiment or company, shall distribute the same to his regiment or company, as he shall deem proper, and require of those to whom they were distributed to return them at such time and place as he shall order and direct; and any officer who shall neglect or refuse to comply with such order, shall forfeit the sum not to exceed double the price of any arms or equipments he shall have received, to be sued for and collected in the name of the commandant of the regiment for the use of the military fund of such regiment.

§ 126. The commanding officer of each regiment shall appoint a suitable person to take charge of the armory, armories, or place of deposit of his regiment, or of the several companies in his regiment, and all arms, equipments, and other property of the State therein deposited, and to discharge all duties connected therewith, as shall be from time to time prescribed by the commanding officer.

§ 127. Such person so appointed shall receive a compensation not to exceed one dollar and fifty cents per day for the time actually employed in cleaning guns and other duties indispensably necessary for the safe keeping and preservation of such property of the State as shall be committed to his charge, which shall be a county charge upon the county in which said armory is situated, and audited and paid in the same manner as other county charges. (*As amended by chap.* 612 *of* 1865.)

§ 128. The commander-in-chief shall, from time to time, make such orders, rules, and regulations as he may deem proper for the observance of all officers having charge of any armory in which arms of the people of this State shall be deposited.

§ 129. Whenever the commissioned officers of any uniformed company in this State shall make application to the commanding officer of their regiment for any arms or equipments suited to the corps to which their company may belong, and who shall, at the same time, furnish such commanding officer with sufficient bonds for the safe keeping and return of the same, he may deliver to such officers such arms and equipments belonging to this State as he shall deem proper; but no such arms or equipments shall be delivered, unless the bonds given for the safe keeping and return thereof shall be approved by the sureties who became responsible in the bonds furnished to the commander-in-chief for all such arms and equipments.

§ 130. Any person who shall willfully injure such armory, or its fixtures, or any gun, sword, pistol, or other property of the State therein deposited, shall be deemed guilty of a misdemeanor.

§ 131. The commissary-general may, from time to time, require any officer to examine any armory provided as aforesaid, and report to him the condition thereof, and of the arms and camp equipage therein deposited.

§ 132. All officers applying for the issue of camp

equipage shall set forth in their application the number of tents which they will require, the time when their respective regiments or companies go into camp, and the number of days which such encampment will continue; and the commanding officer of each camp shall, immediately after the breaking up of the encampment, cause the equipage to be returned to such of the State arsenals, or turned over to such officer as may be directed by the adjutant-general; provided, however, that such tents and camp equipage shall be deposited in some one of the State arsenals on or before the first day of November in each year.

OF THE DRILLS, PARADES, AND RENDEZVOUS OF THE NATIONAL GUARD, AND OF COMPENSATION FOR MILITARY SERVICES.

§ 133. Whenever any company or companies shall be organized, uniformed, and equipped in any regimental district of this State, such company or companies shall parade annually thereafter by regiment, battalion, or company, at such time and place, between the first day of May and the first day of November, as the commanding officers of their respective brigades shall order and direct, for the purpose of discipline, inspection, and review. At any such parade, all the commissioned and non-commissioned officers, musicians, and privates shall appear and discharge any and all the duties required to be performed by the commanding officer. No person shall be permitted in the ranks, on any parade, who does not appear in full uniform, and armed and equipped, suited to the company to which he belongs; and no person shall be permitted in the ranks who is not fully armed and equipped according to the provisions of this act, and the laws of the United States; and all members who shall appear without such arms and equipments, or without a uniform, at any parade, shall be returned as absent from parade and fined accordingly. At such annual parade an actual muster shall be made by the commanding officer present thereat, of each commissioned and non-commissioned officer, musician, and private present and absent, and a muster roll in duplicate, shall be made and officially certified to and returned by such commanding officer, in accordance with such regulations and restrictions as may be issued by the commander-in-chief. And the brigade inspector shall at the same time make a like muster of the field, commissioned, and non-commissioned staff officers of each regiment, separate battalion, or battery; and the said muster rolls shall be filed in the office of the adjutant-general. (*As amended by chap.* 612 *of* 1865.)

§ 134. In addition to the annual inspection herein specified, there shall be six drills or parades of the national guard in each year, not less than three of which shall be by regiment or battalion, and at such times and places as the commander-in-chief, commandant of division, brigade, regiment, or battalion shall direct.

§ 135. The commanding officer, at any parade, may cause those under his command to perform any field or camp duty he shall require; and also to put under guard for the day or time of continuing such parade, any officer, musician, or private who shall disobey the orders of his superior officer, or in any way interrupt the exercises of the day; also all other persons who shall trespass on the parade ground, or in any way or manner interrupt or molest the orderly discharge of duty of those under arms; and also may prohibit and prevent the sale of all spirituous liquors within one mile of such parade or encampment; and also, in his discretion, all hucksters or auction sales, or gambling may be abated as nuisances.

§ 136. In addition to the drills and parades above specified, the commanding officers of companies may require the officers, non-commissioned officers, musicians, and privates of their companies to meet for company drill and parade once in each month, from November to May, and so much oftener as a majority of the members of such company shall prescribe in and by the by-laws for the government of the same.

§ 137. No parade or rendezvous of the national guard shall be ordered on any day during which a general or special election shall be held, nor within five days previous to such election, except in cases of riot, invasion, or insurrection, or of imminent danger thereof; and if any officer shall order any such parade or rendezvous, he shall forfeit and pay to the people of this State the sum of five hundred dollars.

§ 138. For the purpose of warning the non-commissioned officers, musicians, and privates to any parade, encampment, or place of rendezvous, the commandant of each company shall issue his orders, under his hand, to his non-commissioned officers, or to such of them as he may deem proper, requiring them respectively to warn all the non-commissioned officers, musicians, and privates of his company to appear at such parade, encampment, or place of rendezvous, armed and equipped, according to law and regulation.

§ 139. Each non-commissioned officer, to whom such order shall be directed shall warn every person whom he shall therein be required to warn, by reading the orders, or stating the substance thereof in the hearing of such person; or in case of his absence, by leaving a notice thereof at his usual place of abode or business, with some person of suitable age and discretion, or by sending the same to him by mail, directed to him at the post-office nearest his place of residence.

§ 140. Such non-commissioned officer shall make a return to his commandant, in which he shall state the names of all persons by him warned, and the manner of warning them respectively, and shall make oath to the truth of such return, which oath shall be administered by the commandant, and certified by him on the warrant or return.

§ 141. Such commandant shall deliver the return, together with his own return of all delinquencies, to the president of the proper court-martial.

§ 142. The return of such non-commissioned officer, so sworn to and certified, shall be as good evidence on the trial of any person returned as a delinquent, of the facts therein stated, as if such officer had testified to the same before the court-martial on such trial.

§ 143. Every commandant of a company shall make the like return, upon honor, and with like effect, of every delinquency and neglect of duty of his non-commissioned officers, either in not attending on any parade or encampment, or not executing or returning a warrant to them directed, or not obeying the orders of their commanding officers ; and also the names of every non-commissioned officer, musician, or private who shall refuse or neglect to obey the orders of his superior officer, or to perform such military duty or exercise as may be required, or depart from his colors, post, or guard, or leave the ranks without permission from his superior officer.

§ 144. Any commissioned officer of a company may, without a warrant, warn any or all of the members of his company to appear at any parade, encampment, or place of rendezvous. Such warning may be given by him, either personally or by leaving or affixing a notice in the same manner as if given by a non-commissioned officer ; and his certificate, upon honor, shall be received by any court-martial as legal evidence of such warning.

§ 145. Nothing in the provisions of this act shall be so construed as to preclude, in the absence of a proper return, the giving in evidence, at any court-martial upon trial for delinquencies, neglects of duty, or offense whatsoever, matters of fact which go to substantiate the charge or offense ; but all such proof shall be received under the usual rules of evidence in courts of justice.

§ 146. Every non-commissioned officer, musician, and private of the national guard of this State shall be holden to do duty therein for the term of seven years from his enlistment, unless disability after enlistment shall incapacitate him to perform such duty, or he shall be regularly discharged by the commandant of his regiment ; all general and staff officers, all field officers, all commissioned and non-commissioned officers, musicians, and privates, shall be exempt from jury duty during the time they shall perform military duty. No non-commissioned officer, musician, or private in the national guard shall be discharged from service except for physical disability or expiration of term of service. Discharges for physical disability shall be given only upon the certificate of the regimental surgeon ; and no member of any company shall be discharged from service except upon the certificate of the commanding officer of his company, that such member has turned over or satisfactorily accounted for all property issued and charged to him. Commanding officers of regiments shall make returns to the adjutant-general on the first day of January and July of each year, of all discharges granted by them during the previous six months, giving names and grade of the persons so discharged, and the causes for which discharged. (*As amended by chap.* 334 *of* 1864, *and by chap.* 612 *of* 1865.)

§ 147. All notices, warrants, or summons for officers, non-commissioned officers, musicians, and privates of any company or troop, to attend a drill, improvement meeting, or court-martial, may be served either personally or by leaving a written or printed notice, containing the substance of such notice, warrant, or summons, at the dwelling house, store, counting house, or usual place of business of the person to be notified, warned, or summoned, with some person of suitable age and discretion ; and any officer, non-commissioned officer, musician, or private, may also be warned to attend any parade encampment, or drill, by inclosing a notice directed to him at his place of residence, by mail, directed to him at his nearest post-office, at least five days before the service required of him.

§ 148. The officers and non-commissioned staff officers of each regiment shall be warned to attend any parade or drill in the same manner as prescribed by law for the warning of the privates of any company, and the commanding officer of each regiment may designate and order any or all of the non-commissioned staff officers of the regiment to perform that duty, who shall make return thereof to the commanding officer, or the adjutant of the regiment, in the same manner, and under the same penalties for delinquencies, as are by law imposed on non-commissioned officers of companies for similar delinquencies.

§ 149. All orders for encampment, inspection, and review shall be published at least twenty days previous to such parade, in such manner as the commandant of the brigade shall direct, and notice thereof shall at the same time be given to the inspector-general; and all commanding officers of regiments, battalions, or companies may, on any parade, read brigade, regimental, or battalion orders, and notify their several commands to appear as specified in said brigade or regimental order for the purposes therein contained, which notice shall be a sufficient warning to all persons present.

§ 150. Every officer, non-commissioned officer, musician, and private of any uniformed company, who shall unnecessarily neglect to appear on the days at the time and place appointed for such duty, agreeably to the provisions of this act, shall be subject to such fines and penalties as are hereinafter provided.

§ 151. The commanding officer of any brigade, regiment, or battalion, in addition to the rendezvous above prescribed, may require the commissioned officers and non-commissioned officers to meet for exercise and improvement at such times and places as he shall appoint; and he may require them to appear with such arms and accoutrements as he may prescribe; said officers shall thereupon be formed into a corps of instruction, without regard to rank, and shall be thoroughly instructed in the manual of arms, the school of the soldier and company, and in such other theoretical and practical details of duty as the said commanding officer shall deem proper.

§ 152. Each commandant of division may review either one of the brigades in his division in each year; and he shall require the officers of the division staff, armed and equipped as the law and regulation direct, to accompany him.

§ 153. The commandant of each brigade shall attend, with the officers of the brigade staff, armed and equipped as the law and regulation direct, the annual inspection and review of the several regiments and battalions in his brigade.

§ 154. It shall be the duty of the commandants of companies, at the annual inspection, to furnish the brigade inspector with a return which shall show :

1. The number of commissioned, non-commissioned officers, musicians, and privates of his company or troop present on parade, designating the number of each.

2. The number of such company absent from parade.

3. The uniforms, arms, and equipments inspected.

4. The number of uniforms belonging to said company or troop.

5. The arms and equipments in possession of said company or troop.

§ 155. It shall be the duty of each commandant of a regiment or battalion, within twenty days after the annual inspection, to furnish the brigade inspector with a return of the field and staff officers, non-commissioned staff officers, musicians of said regiment or battalion, present and absent, armed and equipped and uniformed according to law and regulation.

§ 156. At all encampments, the brigade inspector shall attend on the first day thereof, to superintend the exercises and manœuvres, and to introduce the system of discipline which is or shall be prescribed by law ; and on such day he shall take the command as drill officer, so far as shall be necessary to the execution of those duties ; and he shall also make an annual inspection at such times as the commanding officer of the brigade shall order and direct.

§ 157. It shall be the duty of the brigade inspector to transmit a copy of the inspection returns annually to the adjutant-general, and a duplicate thereof to the inspector-general, within thirty days after the inspection shall be made. In order to secure a proper accountability for each member, and also for the security of the property issued by the State, the annual inspection and muster rolls of each company and regiment shall be examined and compared by the inspector-general with the muster-in rolls, and the last muster and inspection rolls of the several companies, and the annual fund provided by section one hundred and eighty-three of chapter four hundred and seventy-seven, laws of eighteen hundred and sixty-two, as amended by this act, shall be allowed to such regiments, battalions, and batteries only as shall make a proper return of such rolls ; and upon the certificate of the inspector-general that such rolls make a satisfactory exhibit of the number of the organization and of the State property issued. thereto. There shall be allowed to brigade inspectors as compensation for the annual inspection and muster, and for making proper rolls and returns thereof, the sum of four dollars for each company so inspected and mustered, the same to be allowed and paid in the same manner as other military accounts, upon the certificate of the inspector-general. (*As amended by chap.* 612 *of* 1865, *and by chap.* 809 *of* 1866.)

§ 158. It shall be the duty of the brigade inspector, within thirty days after the annual review in each year, to transmit to the adjutant-general a statement of the reviews and inspection of the several regiments or battalions in his brigade, attended by the commanding officer of division, accompanied by division staff, armed and equipped and uniformed according to law and regulation ; and also the commanding officer of brigade, with the brigade staff, armed and equipped according to law and regulation.

§ 159. In case any general officer or any member of his staff shall neglect to attend such inspection and review, it shall be the duty of the adjutant-general to require such officer to render an excuse in writing to the commander-in-chief for his delinquency. If the commander-in-chief shall deem such excuse insufficient, he shall order a court-martial to try the delinquency.

§ 160. Each uniform company may form by-laws, rules, and regulations, not inconsistent with this act, for the government and improvement of its members in military science; and when approved of by two-thirds of all the members belonging to any such company, shall be binding; but may be altered from time to time as may become necessary.

§ 161. For violations of the by-laws of any uniformed company, the non-commissioned officer, musician, or private offending, by a vote of the company, three-fifths being present, may be expelled from the company; and upon the action of the company being confirmed in orders by the commandant of the regiment, the name of such person or persons shall be stricken from the roll of such company, his certificate of membership shall be surrendered and canceled, and he or they shall cease to be a member or members of such company; and his or their term of service in said company shall not be allowed under the provisions of this act.

§ 162. The adjutant-general shall prescribe the form of enlisting orders to be furnished and used by each company or troop in recruiting or filling up such company or troop with its required number.

§ 163. The commandants of divisions shall discharge the duties, possess the powers, and be liable to the penalties pertaining to their office, as granted by law or military custom, provided that no division parades, except of the first division, or in case of invasion, insurrection, or to aid the civil authorities, shall be ordered without the consent of the commander-in-chief.

§ 164. The commander-in-chief may order such parades or drills of the uniformed troops, or any part of them, as he shall deem proper.

§ 165. There shall be a camp of instruction once in each year after the present year, in each of the division districts of this State, if the commander-in-chief shall so order, to be held at such time and in such manner as he shall direct; and the commander-in-chief is hereby authorized and empowered to order such companies and regiments from such division districts, respectively, to attend such camps as he may deem proper, but in such manner that all the companies and regiments therein shall be ordered to attend such camp from year to year in rotation, provided, always, that not more than ten thousand men in any one year shall be ordered to attend said camps; and in case suitable ground can not be found in any district for said camp, the same may be held in the adjoining district.

§ 166. Such camps shall continue for a period not exceeding ten days, and shall be governed by the rules and regulations of the army of the United States.

§ 167. The commander-in-chief is hereby authorized and empowered, at his discretion, to order such regiments, battalions, batteries, or companies as he shall deem proper, and without regard to arm, not, however, exceeding one thousand men in any one year, to be stationed at such forts or other places as may be furnished by the United States government, or as may be convenient for that purpose within the State of New York, for a period not exceeding ten days in any one year, for instruction in the management of heavy artillery for sea and lake coast defense under such instructors as he shall assign for that purpose.

§ 168. The commander-in-chief shall designate commissioned officers of proper rank without regard to military districts, to command such camps, forts, or other places, and shall assign such other officers, also without regard to military districts, to duty as field and staff officers and instructors, as may be required to fully officer such camps and forts.

§ 169. The commissary-general of ordnance shall furnish, upon the requisition of the commander-in-chief, such arms, ordnance, and ammunition as may be necessary for the use of the military forces so encamped or stationed.

§ 170. The quartermaster-general shall, upon the requisition of the commander-in-chief, furnish such tents, camp equipage, or other State property as may be required for the use of the military forces so encamped or stationed, and shall also furnish the transportation necessary for conveying said forces to and from such camps or stations.

§ 171. The commissary-general of subsistence shall, upon the requisition of the commander-in-chief, provide the subsistence necessary for said forces, such subsistence to conform in price and quantity to the ration prescribed by the general regulations for the army of the United States, and to be issued in kind.

172. The commander-in chief is hereby authorized and empowered to draw his warrant upon the State treasury for such sum as shall be required by the engineer and quartermaster of said camps, forts, or stations, in laying out and preparing the ground designated for such purpose, and in furnishing quarters for said forces and for the services of the officers, instructors, and privates ordered to attend the same; also for all necessary expenses of said forces, including transportation and subsistence; such expenses to be audited by a board to consist of the commander-in-chief, comptroller, State treasurer, and inspector-general.

OF COMPENSATION FOR MILITARY SERVICES.

§ 173. The military forces of this State, when in the actual service of the State in time of war, insurrection, invasion, or imminent danger thereof, shall, during their time of service, be entitled to the same pay, rations, and allowances for clothing, as are or may hereafter be established by law for the army of the United States.

§ 174. There shall be paid to such officers, non-commissioned officers, and privates as shall be specially ordered to attend encampments, and sea and lake coast defense duty, in pursuance of the provisions of this act, not to exceed the following sum each, for every day actually on duty:

1. To all non-commissioned officers, musicians, and privates, one dollar.
2. To all commissioned officers of the line below the rank of captain, two dollars.
3. To all commanding officers of companies, three dollars.

4. To all field officers below the rank of colonel, four dollars.

5. To all commanding officers of regiments, five dollars.

6. To all regimental staff officers, two dollars and fifty cents, and to all non-commissioned staff officers, one dollar and fifty cents.

7. To all brigadier-generals, six dollars.

8. To all brigade staff officers, four dollars.

9. To all major-generals, eight dollars.

10. To all division staff officers, five dollars.

11. All mounted officers, and all members of any company of cavalry or artillery, mounted or equipped, shall receive one dollar per day for each horse actually used by them.

12. To each military storekeeper, such sum, not exceeding twenty-five dollars per annum, as the commander-in-chief shall think proper to allow.

§ 175. The staff of the commander-in-chief and the assistants in the several departments, in lieu of all compensation and allowances now provided by law in time of peace, when upon actual duty under the provisions of this act, either at drills, parades, encampments, lake and sea coast defense duty, or otherwise, shall receive such reasonable and just compensation, not exceeding the full pay and allowances of officers of the same rank in the volunteer services in the United States, as the commander-in-chief shall deem proper, and in no event to exceed the sum of twenty-five hundred dollars per annum, together with their necessary expenses and those of their departments, to be paid by the State upon the certificate of the commander-in-chief, showing a detailed statement of such services and expenses. (*As amended by* § 1, *chap.* 808 *of* 1866.)

§ 176. In case of war, insurrection, rebellion, or invasion, or imminent danger thereof, when the military forces and volunteers of the State of New York, or any part thereof, shall be in the actual service of the State, or in the service of the United States, the staff of the commander-in-chief, while on duty, the assistants and clerks in the several staff departments, and such other officers as may be detailed by the commander-in-chief for the performance of any duties connected with the recruiting, mustering, enrolling, equipping, arming, organizing, paying, inspecting, providing, and administering justice for such forces and volunteers, shall, in lieu of all other allowances under this act, receive such reasonable and just compensation, not exceeding the full pay and allowances of officers of the same rank in the volunteer service of the United States, as the commander-in-chief shall deem proper, together with their necessary expenses and those of their departments, to be paid by the State upon the certificate of the commander-in-chief, showing a detailed statement of such services and expenses. (*As amended by chap.* 612 *of* 1865.)

§ 177. Such clerks shall be employed in the several departments of the general staff of this State as shall be actually necessary for the public service, in the opinion of the commander-in-chief, and they shall receive, for the time they may be actually necessarily employed, such compensation as the commander-in-chief shall prescribe, not exceeding, however, in any case the rate of twelve hundred dollars per annum.

§ 178. The commanding officer of every uniformed company which shall have been ordered into camp, or to perform sea and lake coast defense duty, in accordance with the provisions of this act, shall, at the close of the term for which such company shall have been ordered to such camp or duty, make out an alphabetical list of the members of his company who shall have appeared and performed such duty, uniformed, armed, and equipped as the law and regulations direct, and shall set opposite to each name the number of days each shall have performed duty, and the amount of pay each is entitled to receive for such service and deliver the same, certified on oath to be correct and true, to the commanding officer of the camp or post, who shall immediately cause the same to be transcribed in a book or books to be kept by him for that purpose; such company commandant shall also set forth, opposite to the name of each member of his company, whether such member is indebted to the State in any and what amount on account of his uniform and equipments.

§ 179. The commanding officer of the camp or post shall also, at the close of the time for which each company, battery, battalion, or regiment shall have been ordered to attend for duty thereat, make or cause to be made a complete roster or list of all commissioned officers and non-commissioned staff officers who shall have appeared and performed duty at such parade or encampment, uniformed, armed, and equipped, as the law and regulations direct, and shall set opposite to each name the number of days each shall have performed duty at such encampment or post, and the amount of pay each is entitled to receive for such service, and shall immediately cause the said list to be transcribed in a book or books to be kept by him for that purpose.

§ 180. The commander-in-chief shall draw his warrant upon the comptroller for the amount which shall become due to officers, non-commissioned officers, and privates, for services rendered at the drills and encampments for which payment is allowed by this act.

§ 181. The paymaster-general, or a division or brigade paymaster under his directions, shall, once in each year, visit the different regimental districts of this State, and shall pay to the officers, non-commissioned officers, and privates, such sums as they may be entitled to receive therefor under this act.

§ 182. The commander-in-chief shall have power to prescribe such further rules and regulations to provide for the more convenient payment of all sums which may become due to officers, non-commissioned officers, and privates, under the provisions of this act; and the paymaster-general, under the direction of the commander-in-chief, shall prepare the necessary forms and pay rolls, and cause the same to be transmitted to the commandants of such regiments, camps, and posts.

OF THE REGIMENTAL FUND AND REGIMENTAL BOARDS OF AUDITORS.

§ 183. The comptroller shall annually draw his warrant upon the treasurer in favor of the county treasurer of each county, for the sum of five hundred dollars for each regiment, and the sum of two hundred and fifty dollars for each battalion, and the sum of one hundred dollars for each battery, certified by the adjutant-general, to be organized according to the provisions of this act within the county ; or in case any regiment, battalion, or battery is organized in two or more counties, then the comptroller shall draw his warrant in favor of such county treasurer as the adjutant-general may in his certificate direct, which sums, together with the fines collected from delinquent officers, non-commissioned officers, musicians, and privates, shall constitute the military fund of such regiment, battalion, or battery. (*As amended by* § 5, *of chap.* 425 *of* 1863, *and* § 1, *chap.* 809 *of* 1866.)

§ 184. There shall be a board of officers in each regiment, which shall consist of the commanding officer of the brigade, who shall be president thereof, and of the field officers of the regiment and the senior captain therein, any three of whom shall form a quorum for business, the commanding officer of the brigade being one.

§ 185. The commandant of each brigade shall, from time to time, as he shall deem necessary, convene the board of officers of each regiment created by this act.

§ 186. Such board, when so convened, shall audit all just claims on the military fund of such regiment for contingent expenses of the regiment, and shall make their order on the proper county treasurer, which shall require him to pay such order out of any money in his hands belonging to the military fund of such regiment.

§ 187. Such board may also direct such printing and publishing to be performed and executed as shall be necessary for the best interest of the regiment and service. The members of such board shall be entitled to receive for each day's service, as such members, the sum of two dollars, for not more than three days in any one year, such sum to be certified and paid in the same manner. Such board shall enter their proceedings, from time to time, in a book to be kept for that purpose by each regiment.

§ 188. All county and city treasurers shall report to the brigadier-general, within the bounds of whose brigades he may reside, the amount of all moneys received by them, respectively, by the first days of April and December, annually, and the balance then remaining in their hands, and the number of the regiment to which the same belongs.

OF THE COURTS OF INQUIRY AND COURTS-MARTIAL.

Of the Courts of Inquiry and Courts-Martial for the trial of Officers.

§ 189. Courts of inquiry may be instituted by the commander-in-chief, or the commanding officer of division or brigade, in relation to those officers for whose trial they are authorized to appoint courts-martial, for the purpose of investigating the conduct of any officer, either by his own solicitation, or on a complaint or charge of improper conduct, degrading to the character of an officer, or for the purpose of settling rank; but no such court shall consist of more than one officer, who may, if approved of by the officer ordering the court, require a judge-advocate to attend such court in taking testimony, and in investigating any complaint that may come before such court.

§ 190. Such court shall, without delay, report the evidence adduced, a statement of facts, and an opinion thereon, when required, to the officer instituting such court, who may in his discretion thereupon appoint a court-martial for the trial of the officer whose conduct shall have been inquired into.

§ 191. Every court-martial for the trial of a major-general shall be ordered by the commander-in-chief, and shall consist of five officers, any three of whom shall constitute a quorum.

§ 192. Every court-martial for the trial of a brigadier general shall be ordered by the commander-in-chief, and shall consist of five officers, any three of whom shall constitute a quorum.

§ 193. All other courts-martial for the trial of commissioned officers shall consist of three officers, and shall be ordered, if for the trial of officers above rank of captain, by the commanding officer of division, and for all other officers, by the commanding officer of brigade.

§ 194. No officer arrested shall be brought to trial, unless a copy of the charges and specifications, certified by the officer ordering the arrest, shall be delivered to him, or left at his usual place of abode, within three days after his arrest; nor unless the officer ordering such court-martial shall have ordered the same within thirty days after receiving notice of the arrest, and a copy of the charges and specifications; nor until ten days after a copy of a list of the names of the officers detailed to form the court shall have been delivered to the officer arrested, or left at his usual place of abode.

§ 195. The officer ordering the court may, at any time, supply any vacancy that, from any cause, may happen therein.

§ 196. If the officer accused shall have any cause of challenge to any member of such court, he shall make the same at the time and in the manner provided by the military laws of the United States service and the practice of courts-martial. The arraignment of the accused, the proceedings, trial, and record shall, in all respects, conform to the requirements of the United States law of courts-martial. (*As amended by chap.* 612 *of* 1865.)

§ 197. After the court shall be assembled, and after all challenges, if any are made, shall have been determined, the judge-advocate, whether commissioned or special, shall administer to each member the following oath: " You   do swear (or affirm) that you will faithfully try and determine, according to evidence, the matter now before you, between the State of New York and the prisoner to be tried, and that you will duly administer justice according to the established rules of military law for the government of the military forces of this State, so help you God." (*As amended by chap.* 612 *of* 1865.)

§ 198. Every judge-advocate, whether commissioned or special, and every member of a court-martial, shall keep secret the proceedings and sentence of the court until the same shall be approved or disapproved according to law ; and shall keep secret the vote or opinion of any particular member of the court, unless required to give evidence thereof by a court of justice. (*As amended by chap.* 612 *of* 1865.)

§ 199. The sentence of any such court-martial shall be according to the nature and degree of the offense, and according to military usage, but shall not extend further, in time of peace, than cashiering the officer convicted, and disqualifying him from holding any office in the militia of this State, and imposing a fine not exceeding one hundred dollars.

§ 200. The proceedings and sentence of every court-martial shall, without delay, be delivered to the officer ordering the court, who shall approve or disapprove thereof, within fifteen days thereafter, and shall give notice of his approval or disapproval to the president of such court-martial and to the arresting officer, and he may, at his discretion, publish the sentence, as approved or disapproved, in orders ; but no part of such sentence shall be executed until after the time allowed for appeal has expired.

§ 201. He also shall transmit such proceedings and sentence, and his approval or disapproval thereof, to the adjutant-general, to be kept in his office.

§ 202. The right of appeal to the commander-in-chief, as it now exists by military usage, is reserved ; but no appeal shall be received, unless made within twenty days after the decision appealed from is made known to the person appealing.

§ 203. There shall be allowed and paid out of the treasury, on the certificate of the president and the judge-advocate, on the approval of the judge-advocate-general, to each division, brigade, and special judge-advocate, and to the president and members of any court of inquiry or court-martial for the trial of officers, two dollars for each day actually employed on duty; and the like compensation to every marshal appointed by any such court for every day employed in the execution of the duties required of him. In important cases a reasonable compensation may be paid to any stenographer employed by the court, whose services shall be certified in like manner. (*As amended by chap.* 612 *of* 1865.)

§ 204. The accounts of all persons who, under this article, are entitled to be paid out of the treasury, shall be audited by the comptroller, who shall, on the application of the governor, draw his warrant on the treasurer for such sum of money as may be requisite in the execution of the provisions of this act; and may require the chief of each staff department to account quarterly for all money received by him for the purpose connected with his department.

Of Regimental and Battalion Courts-Martial.

§ 205. The commandant of each brigade may at any time appoint a regimental or battalion court-martial for any regiment or battalion in his brigade, to consist, if practicable, of a field officer or captain.

§ 206. The appointment of said court shall be published in orders at least three weeks previous to the convening of the court; and the officer appointing said court shall fix the day on which it shall convene, and when convened, the court may adjourn from time to time as shall become necessary for the transaction of business, but the whole session of the court, from the day on which it shall convene until its dissolution, shall not exceed three weeks.

§ 207. In case any vacancy shall happen in the court,

or a new court shall be required, the officer ordering the court, or his successor in command, may fill such vacancy or order a new court.

§ 208. The officer constituting such court, before he shall enter on his duties as such, shall take the following oath:

"I,   , do swear that I will well and truly try and determine, according to evidence, all matters between the people of the State of New York and any person or persons which shall come before the regimental (or battalion) court martial to which I have been appointed."

§ 209. Such oath shall be taken by the president, on or before the day on which the court shall convene, before a justice of the county in which he may reside, or a field officer of his regiment or battalion; and it shall be the duty of such justice or field officer to administer the oath without fee or reward.

§ 210. Such court shall direct a non-commissioned officer, or other fit person or persons, to be by him designated, to summon all delinquents and parties accused to appear before the court, at a time and place to be by him appointed, which service shall be personal, or by leaving such summons at the residence of such parties.

§ 211. Such non-commissioned officer, or other person or persons so designated, shall make the like return, and with like effect, as commissioned and non-commissioned officers are authorized and required to make, in cases of warning to a company or regimental parade, and shall be subject to the like penalties for neglect of duty.

§ 212. The court, when organized, shall have the trial of all offenses, delinquencies, and deficiencies, in the regiment or battalion for which it shall have been called, and shall have power to impose and direct to be levied all the fines to which non-commissioned officers, musicians, or privates are declared to be subject by the provisions of this act.

§ 213. From the sentence of any such court, imposing a fine for any offense, delinquency, or deficiency, an appeal, if made within twenty days, shall be allowed to the officer instituting the court, or to his successor in command, who may remit or mitigate such penalty or fine.

§ 214. There shall be allowed and paid out of the military fund of said regiment:

1. To the officer constituting said court, a sum equal to one day's pay for field duty for each day he may be actually employed in holding the court or engaged in the business thereof, or in traveling to or from the court, allowing thirty miles for a day's travel.

2. To the non-commissioned officer or other person who shall have summoned delinquents to appear before the court, one dollar and twenty-five cents for each day he may have been necessarily so employed, and the same sum for each day of his attendance on the court.

3. Each officer to whom a warrant for the collection of fines may be directed, shall be entitled to the same fees, and be subject to the same penalties for any neglect, as are allowed and provided for on executions issued out of justices' courts.

4. For all other services and commitments under this act, the sheriff, jailer, and constables executing the same shall be entitled to the like fees as for similar services in other cases.

§ 215. All fines and penalties imposed by any regimental or battalion court-martial, shall be paid, by the officer collecting the same, to the treasurer of the county within which the officer instituting the court may reside, and shall belong to the military fund of such regiment.

OF THE IMPOSITION OF PENALTIES AND FINES FOR VIOLATING THE PROVISIONS OF THIS ACT.

§ 216. In time of peace, every commissioned officer, for disobedience of orders, neglect or ignorance of duty, unofficerlike conduct or disrespect to a superior officer, or for neglecting to furnish himself with a uniform and equipments within six months after receiving his commission, shall be arrested and brought to trial before a court-martial, who may, on conviction, sentence him to be cashiered, incapacitated from holding any military commission, or fined to an amount not exceeding one hundred dollars, or to be reprimanded, or may sentence him to all or either of such penalties, in their discretion.

§ 217. Every commissioned officer refusing to pay over moneys in his hands, as is directed by the provisions of this act, shall be liable to be tried and cashiered, or otherwise punished therefor, by a court-martial.

§ 218. Every commissioned officer, and every noncommissioned officer, musician, and private, shall, on due conviction, be subject for the following offenses, to the fines thereto annexed:

1. Every non-commissioned officer, musician, and private, for non-appearance, when duly warned or summoned, at a company parade, a fine of two dollars; at a regimental or battalion parade or encampment, not less than three nor more than six dollars; and at a place of rendezvous, when called into actual service, a sum not exceeding twelve months' pay, nor less than one month's pay.

2. Every commissioned officer, for non-attendance at any parade or encampment, and every such officer, noncommissioned officer, musician, and private, neglecting or refusing to obey the orders of his superior officers on any day of parade or encampment, or to perform such military duty or exercise as may be required or departing from his colors, post, or guard, or leaving his place or ranks without permission, a fine not more than one hundred nor less than five dollars.

3. For neglecting or refusing to obey any order or warrant to him lawfully given or directed, or to make a proper return thereof, if such return be necessary, or making a false return, or neglecting or refusing when required, to summon a delinquent before a court-martial, or duly to return such summons, a fine not more than one hundred nor less than five dollars.

§ 219. Every commissioned officer, for neglecting or

refusing to act as such when duly elected and commismissioned, may be sentenced to pay a fine not less than ten dollars; every non-commissioned officer, for neglecting or refusing to act as such, when duly appointed and warranted, may be sentenced to pay a fine not less than five dollars; and every non-commissioned officer, for neglect of duty or disorderly or unofficerlike conduct, in addition to other penalties, may be reduced to the ranks by the commandant of the company, with the approbation of the commandant of the regiment or battalion.

§ 220. Every non-commissioned officer, musician, or private, who shall unlawfully discharge any fire-arms within two miles of any parade, on the day thereof, shall be sentenced to pay a fine of one dollar.

§ 221. Any commissioned officer who shall retain a commission received by him for any subaltern for more than thirty days, without giving notice by mail or otherwise to the person entitled to it, shall be liable to pay a fine not exceeding twenty-five dollars, to be imposed by the proper court-martial on the complaint of any officer interested. In addition to the penalties imposed by any of the provisions of this act, every commissioned and non-commissioned officer, musician, and private of a company or troop, or any other person who shall appear at any parade or encampment wearing any personal disguise or other unusual or ludicrous article of dress, or any arms, weapons, or other implements not required by law, and calculated to excite ridicule, or to interrupt the orderly and peaceable discharge of duty by those under arms, shall be liable to a fine of not more than twenty-five and not less than five dollars, to be imposed by the proper court-martial.

§ 222. The court-martial by which any delinquent is tried may excuse such delinquent, if it shall be made satisfactorily to appear to the court that he has a reasonable excuse for such delinquency.

§ 223. No action shall be maintained against any member of a court-martial, or officer, or agent acting under its authority, on account of the imposition of a fine, or the execution of a sentence on any person, if such person shall have been returned as a delinquent and duly summoned, and shall have neglected to appear and render his excuse for such delinquency, or show his exemption before such court.

§ 224. When a suit or proceeding shall be commenced in any court by any person against any officer of this State, for any act done by such officer in his official capacity, in the discharge of any duty under this act, or against any person acting under authority or order of any such officer, or by virtue of any warrant issued by him pursuant to law, or against any collector or receiver of taxes, the defendant may require the plaintiff in such suit to file security for the payment of the costs that may be incurred by the defendant in such suit or proceeding, and the defendant, in all cases, may plead the general issue, and give the special matter in evidence, and in case the plaintiff shall be non-prossed or non-suited, or have a verdict or judgment against him, the defendant shall recover treble costs.

OF THE COLLECTION OF FINES AND PENALTIES.

§ 225. For the purpose of collecting such fines as may be imposed by any court-martial authorized by this act, the president of the court shall, within thirty days after the fines have been imposed, make a list of all the persons fined, designating the company to which they respectively belong, and the sums imposed as fines on each person, and shall draw his warrant, under his hand and seal, directed to any marshal, sheriff, or constable of any city or county (as the case may be), thereby commanding him to levy such fines, together with the costs of the goods and chattels of such delinquents. No property shall be exempt from the payment of such fines, *and in default of sufficient goods and chattels with which to satisfy the same, then to take the body of such delinquent and convey him to the common jail of such city or county.* Payment of all fines imposed by any court-martial organized pursuant to the provisions of this act, for the trial of officers, may be enforced in like manner. (*As amended by chap. 612 of* 1865, *and by* § 1, *chap.* 809 *of* 1866.)

§ 226. It shall be the duty of the jailer to whom such delinquent may be delivered, to keep him closely confined, without bail or mainprize, for two days, for any fine not exceeding two dollars, and two additional days for every dollar above that sum, unless the fine, together with the costs and the jailer's fees, shall sooner be paid; but no non-commissioned officer, musician, or private shall be imprisoned for the non-payment of such fine or fines for a period exceeding ten days. (*As amended by chap.* 612 *of* 1865.)

§ 227. Every such marshal, sheriff, or constable, to whom any list and warrant shall be directed and delivered, may execute the same by levying and collecting the fines within forty days from the receipt of such warrant, and make return thereof to the officers who issued the same. (*As amended by* § 8 *of chap.* 612 *of* 1865.)

§ 229. Any warrant for the collection of fines, issued by virtue of this chapter, shall and may be renewed in the same manner that executions issued from justices' courts may by law be renewed.

§ 230. The amount of any fines so collected shall be paid, by the officer collecting the same, into the county treasury, and shall form a portion of, and be credited to, the regimental fund of the regiment to which the person so fined belonged.

§ 231. In addition to the bond now required by law to be given by the marshal, sheriff, constable, or other officer, for the faithful discharge of his duties, such named officers shall execute a bond for the payment of all moneys by them collected, under the provisions of this act; and the sureties of such officers, hereby authorized to collect fines and penalties, shall be liable for any official delinquency under this act, such bonds to be approved by the county judge of each county.

OF THE STATE OF NEW YORK. 171

GENERAL PROVISIONS APPLICABLE TO ALL COURTS-
MARTIAL AND COURTS OF INQUIRY.

§ 232. The president of every court-martial, and of every court of inquiry, both before and after he shall have been sworn, and also the judge-advocate, if required, shall issue subpœnas for all witnesses whose attendance at such court may, in his opinion, be necessary in behalf of the people of this State, and also on application for all witnesses in behalf of any officer charged or accused, or persons returned as delinquent; and may direct the commandment of any company to cause such subpœna to be served on any witness or member of his company.

§ 233. The president of such court-martial, or the court of inquiry, shall have power to administer the usual oath to witnesses, and shall have the same power to compel attending witnesses to be sworn and testify, and to preserve order, as courts of common law jurisdiction; and all sheriffs, jailers, and constables are hereby required to execute any precept issued by such president or court for that purpose.

§ 234. Every witness not appearing in obedience to such subpœna when duly served personally with a copy of the same, and not having a sufficient or reasonable excuse, shall forfeit to the people of this State a sum not less than ten nor more than fifty dollars; and the president of such court shall, from time to time, report to the district attorney the names of all such delinquent witnesses, together with the names and places of residence of the persons serving such subpœna, the better to enable him to prosecute for such forfeiture.

§ 235. Whenever it shall appear to the satisfaction of any court-martial or court of inquiry, by proof made before such court, that any person duly subpœnaed to appear as a witness before said court, shall have refused or neglected, without just cause, to attend as such witness, in conformity to such subpœna, and the party in whose behalf such witness shall have been subpœnaed shall make oath that the testimony of such witness is material, such court, or the president thereof, shall have power to issue an attachment to compel the attendance of such witness.

§ 236. Every such attachment shall be executed in the same manner as a warrant, and by any officer authorized to execute warrants, and the fees of the officers serving the same shall be paid by the person against whom the same shall have been issued, unless he shall show reasonable cause, to the satisfaction of such court, for his omission to attend; such costs shall be ascertained by the court, who may thereupon issue an execution for the collection against the person liable to pay the same, and which may be collected as other executions are collected, and by any officer authorized to collect executions issued from courts of justice.

§ 237. Any person or persons who shall be guilty of disorderly, contemptuous, or insolent behavior in, or use any insulting or contemptuous or indecorous language or expressions to, or before any court-martial or court of inquiry, or any member of either of such courts, in open court, intending to intercept the proceedings or to impair the respect, the authority of such courts, may be committed to the jail of the county in which said courts shall sit, by warrant under the hand and seal of the president of such court.

§ 238. Such warrant shall be directed to the sheriff or any or either of the constables and marshals of any such county, or any officer attending the court, and shall set forth the particular circumstances of the offense adjudged to have been committed; and shall command the officer to whom it is directed to take the body of such person and commit him to the jail of the county, there to remain without bail or mainprize, in close confinement for a time to be limited not exceeding three days, and until the officer's fees for committing and the jailer's fees be paid.

§ 239. Such sheriff shall receive the body of any person who shall be brought to him by virtue of such warrant, and keep him until the expiration of the time mentioned in the warrant, and until the officer's and jailer's fees shall be paid, or until the offender shall be discharged by due course of law, unless sooner discharged by any judge of a court of record, in the same manner and under the same rules as in cases of imprisonment under process for contempt from a court at law.

§ 240. In the absence of the president of any court-martial, the senior officer present may preside, with all the powers of the president; and all the members of such court shall, when on duty, be in full uniform.

§ 241. The president of any court-martial or any court of inquiry may appoint, by warrant under his hand and seal, one or more marshals.

§ 242. The marshals so appointed may not only perform the usual duties of such marshals, but may also execute all process lawfully issued by such president or court, and perform all acts and duties in this act imposed on and authorized to be performed by any sheriff, marshal, or constable.

§ 243. Whenever the sentence of any regimental or battalion court-martial shall be appealed from, the officer hearing the appeal shall require the court, or the president thereof, to furnish him forthwith with a statement of the case, and of the evidence touching the same; which statement and evidence shall, in the case of an appeal to the commanding officer of the brigade, be forthwith, on notice of such appeal, transmitted to him. (*As amended by chap.* 612 *of* 1865.)

§ 244. Such statement being furnished, the officer hearing the appeal may hear such further evidence, by affidavit or otherwise as the nature of the case may require, and for that purpose he shall have power to administer oaths to witnesses produced before him, and order depositions of such witnesses as can not reasonably be produced at the hearing of such appeal. (*As amended by chap.* 612 *of* 1865.)

§ 245. The last two sections shall extend to appeals

made from the order of an officer approving the sentence of a court-martial.

§ 246. If any officer having a warrant for the collection of any fine shall not be able to collect the fine within the time specified therein, then the officers issuing the warrant may, at any time thereafter, within two years from the time imposing the fines, issue a new warrant against any delinquent, or renew the former warrant, from time to time as may become necessary.

§ 247. Any warrant for the collection of fines, issued by virtue of this act, shall and may be renewed in the same manner that executions, issued from justices' courts, may by law be renewed.

§ 248. It shall be the duty of the respective presidents of courts-martial to prosecute, in the name of the people of the State of New York, any marshal, or constable, sheriff, and their sureties, who shall incur any penalty for neglect in the execution or return of any warrant, or in paying over moneys collected by him.

§ 249. Whenever any court-martial shall consist of one person, he shall be deemed the president thereof, within the meaning of this act.

§ 250. The chiefs of the staff in each division, regiment, or battalion, shall, on or before the first day of November, in each year, return to the commandants of division and brigade, respectively, the names of all commissioned officers absent from any parade, encampment, or drill, which they shall be required by law to attend. Within ten days after the receipt of such returns, the respective commandants of division or brigade, as the case may be, shall order a court-martial, to consist of three commissioned officers, without regard to rank, to pass upon such delinquency. It shall not be necessary to cause the arrest of such absentee, nor to serve any charges, unless, in the discretion of the officer ordering the court, it may be proper; but the delinquent may be fined, pursuant to the provisions of this act, provided notice of the return and of the time appointed for holding the court-martial shall have been delivered to him or left at his usual place of abode, at least ten days before the assembling of said court.

§ 251. The court may excuse any such delinquent for good cause shown. (*As amended by chap.* 612 *of* 1865.)

§ 252. Any fine for offenses against the by-laws of any company of the national guards or of regimental boards, not exceeding the sum of twenty-five dollars, a certified copy of the proceedings relating to the infliction of which has been returned to any regimental court-martial or court of appeals, may be enforced by such court in the manner hereinbefore provided, due notice being given to the delinquent; and further provided, that a certified copy of said by-laws be filed with the commandant of the regiment.

§ 253. Whenever any portion of the military forces of this State shall be ordered to assemble for purposes of military instruction, under the authority of the commander-in-chief, or whenever any part of the State forces shall be ordered to assemble, under his authority, in time of war, insurrection, invasion, or public danger, the rules and articles of war, and general regulations for the government of the army of the United States, so far as they are applicable, and with such modifications as the commander-in-chief may prescribe, shall be considered in force and regarded as a part of this act, during the continuance of such instruction, and to the close of such state of war, invasion, insurrection, or public danger; but no punishment under such rules and articles which shall extend to the taking of life, shall, in any case, be inflicted, except in time of actual war, invasion, or insurrection, declared by proclamation of the governor to exist.

OF THE DUTIES OF CERTAIN STAFF OFFICERS, AND OF VARIOUS MATTERS CONNECTED WITH THEIR VARIOUS RESPECTIVE DEPARTMENTS.

Of the Adjutant-General.

§ 254. The adjutant-general shall keep a roster of all

the officers of the military forces of this State, containing the date of their commissions, their rank, the corps to which they belong, the division, brigade, and regiment of such corps, and the places of their residence, as accurately as can be ascertained; which roster shall be revised and corrected every year.

§ 255. He shall also enter in a book, to be kept for that purpose, a local description of the several company, regimental, brigade, and division districts.

§ 256. It shall be the duty of the commandants of divisions and brigades to furnish the adjutant-general with a roster of their officers, containing the facts requisite to enable him to comply with the provisions of this act.

§ 257. The books required by the adjutant-general to comply with this act, shall be furnished him at the expense of this State, and shall go to his successors in office.

§ 258. The seal now used in the office of the adjutant-general shall continue to be the seal of his office, and shall from time to time be delivered to his successor in office; and all copies of records or papers in his office, duly certified and authenticated under the said seal, shall be evidence in all cases, in like manner as if the originals were produced.

§ 259. It shall be the duty of the adjutant-general to cause so much of the militia laws as shall at any time be in force to be printed in proper form, from time to time, and to distribute one copy to each commissioned officer, and to each town clerk, supervisors' clerk, and county treasurer in this State; and also, to prepare and cause all necessary blank books, forms, and notices to be transmitted at the expense of this State, to carry into full effect the provisions of this act; and the comptroller is hereby directed to draw his warrant on the treasurer of this State for the expenses incurred under this section.

§ 260. The adjutant-general is hereby authorized to appoint an assistant, who shall have the rank of colonel and be commissioned by the commander-in-chief, and who shall hold such office during the pleasure of the adjutant-general. In case of absence of the adjutant-general from the city of Albany, or in case of his inability to perform his duties, his assistant shall have full power to perform all the duties appertaining to the office of the adjutant-general. But nothing in this section shall be so construed as to give any validity to the acts of said assistant, or to those of any acting assistant, in case of the disapproval of the adjutant-general, after such disapproval shall have been shown by special order to that effect. (*As amended by chap.* 612 *of* 1865.)

Of the Commissary-General.

§ 261. The commissary-general shall keep in good repair the arsenals and magazines of the State, and attend to the due preservation and safe keeping, cleaning, and repairing of the ordnance, arms, accoutrements, ammunition, munitions of war, and implements of every description, the property of this State; and he shall at all times have the control and disposition of the same for that purpose.

§ 262. He shall, under the direction of the commander-in-chief, dispose, to the best advantage, of all damaged powder, and of all ordnance, arms, ammunition, accoutrements, tools, implements, and warlike stores of every kind whatsoever, that shall be deemed unsuitable for the use of the State.

§ 263. He shall, from time to time, render a just and true account of all sales made by him, with all convenient speed, to the governor, and shall pay the proceeds of such sale into the treasury of the State for military purposes, or expend the same in the purchase of suitable arms, ammunition, and camp or other equipage, as the commander-in-chief may direct.

§ 264. Whenever the commanding officer of a brigade shall certify that a stand of colors, or any drums, fifes, or bugles are necessary for any company, battalion, or regiment in his brigade, the commissary-general, with the approbation of the commander-in-chief, shall furnish such company, battalion, or regiment with a stand of colors, and a sufficiency of drums, fifes, and bugles, at the expense of the State.

§ 265. The commissary-general shall issue the proper allowance of powder and balls to artillery companies for practice ; and the several commandants of artillery companies shall annually report to the commissary-general the situation and state of the pieces of ordnance, arms, implements, and accoutrements, the property of the State, intrusted to their charge respectively.

§ 266. The commissary-general shall issue all ammunition, suited to the several arms of the service, upon the requisition of any commandant of brigade, regiment, or battalion ; and shall, on a like requisition, replace such articles or implements for ordnance as may be by use rendered unfit for service.

§ 267. The commissary-general shall report annually to the commander-in-chief, whose duty it shall be to transmit the same to the legislature, a true and particular statement, showing the actual situation and disposition of all the ordnance, arms, ammunition, and other munitions of war, property or things, which in any wise appertain to or respect the department confided to his keeping.

§ 268. He shall keep a just and true account of all the expenses necessarily incurred in and about his department, which shall include all expenses for transportation to and from the arsenals, all ordnance, arms, ammunition, and camp equipage, and deliver the same to the comptroller, who shall thereupon examine and audit the same, and shall draw his warrant on the treasurer for such sum as he shall audit and certify to be due.

§ 269. It shall be the duty of the judge-advocate-general to prosecute any bond, the condition of which is violated by a neglect or refusal of any officer to report the condition of any arms or equipage, or to return the same to any of the arsenals of this State, as required by law.

§ 270. The commissary-general is authorized to appoint an assistant, with the rank of colonel, and who shall be commissioned by the commander-in-chief, and hold his office during the pleasure of the commissary-general, and shall perform the duties now required by law to be performed by the military storekeeper at the New York arsenal, and shall be compensated in the same manner as such military storekeeper has been compensated. In the absence of the commissary-general from the city of New York, or in case of his inability to perform his duties, his assistant shall have full power to perform all the duties appertaining to the office of the commissary-general; but nothing in this section shall be so construed as to give any validity to the acts of such assistant in case of the disapproval of the commissary-general.

Of the Inspector-General.

§ 271. It shall be the duty of the inspector-general to visit, at least once in every two years, each regimental district in the State. He shall critically inspect, as often as he may deem necessary, every branch connected with the military service, including armories, arsenals, and military storehouses; and he shall also attend to the organization of the militia, and report to general headquarters the improvement in discipline and tactical instruction of the uniformed forces.

§ 272. Commandants of regiments and companies shall furnish to the inspector-general such information as he may require, as to the number and kinds of arms, equipments, and military property of the State issued to their respective regiments and companies; and, at the conclusion of the inspection of any armory, arsenal, or military storehouse, if he find the property which ought to be kept therein, or any part of it, missing, injured, unfit for use, or deficient in any respect, he shall forthwith report the facts, in respect thereto, to the commander-in-chief.

§ 273. It shall be his duty, after the first day of November in each year, to inspect the tents and camp equipage belonging to the State, and report any deficiency therein, or any damaged property or unfit for use, to the commander-in-chief on or before the first day of January next thereafter. Upon receiving the reports mentioned in this and the last preceding section, the commander-in-chief may order such property to be sold at public auction, upon thirty days' notice to be published once a week in the State paper, and also in some newspaper printed in the county in which such property is situated, to the highest bidder, under the direction of the commissary-general of ordnance, and the net avails thereof shall be paid into the treasury to the credit of the militia fund. (*As amended by chap.* 612 *of* 1865.)

§ 274. In his annual report he shall state what general and field officers have been in command of parades and encampments, what changes of general or field officers have been made, and what degree of improvement has been attained by both officers and men, and whether the general regulations have been observed, together with such suggestions as he may see fit to make.

§ 275. To the inspector-general will be referred, by order of the commander-in-chief, such matters as require an examination at a distance from the general headquarters, for the information of the commander-in-chief; and it shall be the duty of inspector-general, upon such reference, to report upon the qualifications of persons named to the commander-in-chief, for appointment to military office, and also upon the possession of the necessary requisites by the applicants for the organization of companies.

§ 276. The division and brigade inspectors, whenever required by the inspector-general, shall report to him the condition of their respective divisions or brigades, and shall also, upon his request, report to him upon any matter properly belonging to his department, which may require examination within their respective division or brigade districts.

§ 277. The inspector-general shall visit the several encampments which shall be ordered by the commander-in-chief, and to ascertain whether the troops have been properly instructed in the exercises and evolutions of the field ; he will cause them to be exercised in the manœuvres required to be practiced during the year, as prescribed by the regulations ; and he will give his instructions, as to the exercises, to the commanding officer, who will issue all necessary orders and directions to the troops for their execution.

§ 278. The inspector-general shall, at least once in every two years, examine the book of proceedings of the board of auditors of each regiment, and the accounts filed with the secretary of such board during the two years previous, or since the last examination made by the inspector-general, and he shall carefully compare the book of proceedings with accounts ; he shall also examine the warrants drawn by the board of auditors, in the possession of the county treasurer, and he shall specially report to the commander-in-chief whether the proceedings of the board of auditors are regularly and properly entered, and whether the warrants are in due form ; and whether any military funds have been drawn from the county treasurer for improper purposes, or by persons not entitled thereto.

§ 279. The inspector-general is hereby authorized to appoint an assistant, who shall have the rank of colonel, and be commissioned by the commander-in-chief, and who shall hold such office during the pleasure of the inspector-general, and shall receive the same compensation as the assistant adjutant-general. In the absence of the inspector-general from the city of Albany, or in case of his inability to perform his duties, his assistant shall have full power to perform all duties appertaining to the office of the inspector-general. But nothing in this section shall be so construed as to give any validity to the acts of said assistant, in case of the disapproval of the inspector-general.

Of the Judge-Advocate-General.

§ 280. The judge-advocate-general, as chief of his

department, is charged with the supervision, care, and management of all things relating to the administration of justice among the military forces of this State. He shall diligently scrutinize and examine the proceedings of all courts-martial where an appeal has been taken, and report thereon for the information of the commander-in-chief; he shall also, in like manner, report in all cases of disputed elections where an appeal has been taken. Under the orders of the commander-in-chief, the judge-advocate-general shall act as judge-advocate at any court-martial where the public interests shall require his attendance.

§ 281. The judge-advocate-general is the legal adviser of the several staff departments, upon all legal questions which may arise therein, and to him may be referred for supervision all contracts, agreements, or other instruments, to be drawn or executed in the course of the business of such department.

§ 282. The officers of the judge-advocate-general's department, when not engaged in the special duties of the same, may be detailed for such other staff duty as the commandants of their respective brigades or divisions shall direct.

OF INVASION, INSURRECTION, BREACHES OF THE PEACE, AND DRAFTS OF THE MILITIA.

Of Invasion and Insurrection.

§ 283. In cases of insurrection or invasion, or imminent danger thereof, the commander-in-chief may, by proclamation or otherwise, order and direct the commandants of such company districts as he shall designate, to accept sufficient volunteers, should the same offer, to raise said company, and maintain the same at the maximum number provided by law, and if sufficient volunteers should not offer, then a sufficient number shall be drafted from the reserve militia of said districts in the manner hereinafter provided, who shall thereupon be enrolled as national guards in said company, and shall be liable to duty in case the military forces of the State should be called into service.

§ 284. The commander-in-chief shall have power, in case of insurrection or invasion, or imminent danger thereof, to order into the service of the State such number and description of companies or regiments of the national guard, or of other militia of the State as he shall deem proper, and under the command of such officers as he shall direct, and in such case the forces so called into service shall receive the same pay and rations as troops in the service of the United States. And all the acts, proclamations, and orders of the governor of this State since the sixteenth day of April, eighteen hundred and sixty-one, relating to the calling out of the militia or volunteers from this State for the service of the United States, are hereby approved, and in all respects legalized and made valid, to the same intent and with the same effect as if they had been issued and done with the previous express authority and direction of the legislature of this State, and all commissions issued or hereafter to be issued to the officers of such volunteer forces by the governor of this State, in accordance with the act of congress in such cases made and provided, are hereby confirmed.

§ 285. In case of any invasion, or of imminent danger thereof, within the limits of any division, brigade, regiment, or battalion, it shall be the duty of the commandant of such division, brigade, regiment, or battalion, to order out, for the defense of the State, the militia, or any part thereof, under his command, and immediately report what he has done to the commander-in-chief, through the adjutant-general.

§ 286. It shall also be his duty to give immediate notice of such invasion, and of the circumstances attending the same, to his immediate commanding officer, by whom such information shall be transmitted with the utmost expedition to the commander-in-chief.

§ 287. The commandant of every regiment or battalion, within the limits of which an insurrection may happen, shall immediately assemble his regiment or battalion, under arms, and with the utmost expedition shall transmit information of such insurrection to the commandant of his brigade and to the commander-in-chief.

§ 288. He shall also give immediate notice of such insurrection to any judge of the county in which it shall happen, and shall take such measures for its suppression as to such judge shall appear most proper and effectual.

§ 289. If the said judge shall deem a greater force requisite to quell the insurrection, he shall require such additional force as he may deem necessary from the commandant of the division, or of any brigade therein, whose duty it shall be to obey his requisition.

§ 290. Every person who, whilst in the actual service of this State, shall be wounded or disabled in opposing or suppressing any invasion or insurrection, shall be taken care of and provided for at the expense of the State.

OF RIOTS, TUMULTS, BREACHES OF THE PEACE, AND RESISTANCE TO PROCESS.

§ 291. In case of any breach of the peace, tumult, riot, or resistance to process of this State, or apprehension of imminent danger of the same, it shall be lawful for the sheriff of any county, or the mayor of any city, to call for aid from any division, brigade, regiment, battalion, or company; and it shall be the duty of the commanding officer of such division, brigade, regiment, battalion, or company, to whom such order is given, to order out, in aid of the civil authorities, the military force, or any part thereof, under his command.

§ 292. In such case it shall not be necessary for commandants of companies to issue written orders or notices for calling out their men, but verbal orders and notices shall be sufficient.

§ 293. It shall be the duty of the commanding officer

of any division, brigade, regiment, battalion, or company, in all cases when so called into service, to provide the men of his command, so ordered out, with at least twenty-four rounds of ball cartridge, and arms in complete order for actual service.

§ 294. Such officer shall be subject, as provided by law, to the sheriff or public officer who shall so require his aid ; and for refusing or neglecting to obey the order of such sheriff, or public officer so requiring service, or for interfering or in any way hindering or preventing the men of his command from performing such duty, or in any manner, by neglect or delay, preventing the due execution of law, every such commanding officer, and every commissioned officer under his command so offending, shall be liable to a fine of not less than one hundred nor more than five hundred dollars, and imprisonment in the county jail for a period not exceeding six months.

§ 295. It shall be the duty of the district attorney of any county where such offense shall be committed, to prosecute the same ; and in addition thereto, such officer shall be liable to be tried by court-martial and sentenced to be cashiered and incapacitated forever after for holding military commission in this State.

§ 296. Any non-commissioned officer, musician, or private, who shall neglect or refuse to obey the orders of his commanding officer in the case above provided for, shall be liable to a fine of not less than twenty-five nor more than one hundred dollars, and imprisonment in the county jail for a period not to exceed three months, to be prosecuted and recovered in the manner hereinbefore provided in the case of commissioned officers.

§ 297. All officers, non-commissioned officers, and privates, in cases of riot, tumult, breach of the peace, resistance to process, or whenever called upon in aid of the civil authorities, shall receive the compensation provided by an act entitled, " An act to enforce the laws and preserve order," passed April 15th, eighteen hundred and forty-five, which continues in force, and shall be published with this act; and every person who shall be wounded or disabled in such service, shall be taken care of and provided for at the expense of the county where such service shall be rendered.

OF DRAFTS OF THE MILITIA.

§ 298. Whenever the commander-in-chief shall order a draft from the reserved militia of any company district, to raise the company of the national guard therein to, and maintain the same at, either the minimum or maximum number provided by this act, or whenever a general draft of the militia shall be made by order of the commander-in-chief, or of the president of the United States, such draft shall be determined by lot, to be drawn by the clerk of the county in which such roll has been filed, in the presence of the county judge and the mayor of any city, or the supervisor of any town or ward, upon the requisition of the commanding officer of the regiment within whose bounds such person may reside.

§ 299. Any person so drafted may, within ten days after receiving such notice of the same, present to the commandant of the regiment, independent battery, or battalion, his certificate of exemption by reason of physical disability, from some surgeon or assistant-surgeon of the national guard, or other due and sufficient proof of his non-liability to military duty, and if such certificate or proof shall be sufficient and satisfactory, such person shall be discharged and another person shall be drafted in his stead, in accordance with the provisions of this act. The necessary expenses for serving notices upon drafted persons shall be a county charge upon the county in which such drafted persons shall reside respectively, and shall be audited and paid in the same manner as other county charges are audited and paid. (*As amended by chap.* 612 *of* 1865.)

§ 300. Any person so drafted, in accordance with the above provisions, may offer a substitute at the time of the rendezvous of the drafted military force and militia, and such substitute, if he shall be an able-bodied man, of the age of twenty-one years and upward, and shall consent in writing to subject himself to all the duties, fines, forfeitures, and punishments to which his principal would have been subject had he personally served, shall be accepted,by the commandant of the company of drafted militia to which his principal may belong.

Any person so drafted, who may be a member of any religious denomination whatever, as from scruples of conscience may be averse to bearing arms, shall be excused from said draft on payment to the clerk of the county by whom such draft is made the sum of three hundred dollars, to be by said county clerk paid to the comptroller of the State, to be applied to the purposes mentioned in this act. (*As amended by* § 6, *chap.* 425 *of* 1863.)

§ 301. Whenever the president of the United States or the commander-in-chief shall order a draft from the militia for public service, such draft shall be made in the following manner :

1. When the draft required to be made shall be a number equal to one or more companies to each brigade, such draft shall be made by company, to be determined by lot, to be drawn by the commandant of brigade in the presence of the commanding officers of the regiments composing said brigade, from the military forces of the State in his brigade, organized, uniformed, armed, and equipped, according to the provisions of this act.

2. In case such draft shall require a number equal to one regiment, such shall be determined by lot in the manner above prescribed.

3. In case such draft shall require a larger number than the whole number of men composing the military force of said brigade, such additional draft shall be made of the requisite number, to supply such deficiency, from the military roll of the reserve militia of each town

or ward, filed in the office of the city, village, or town clerk, as hereinbefore provided.

§ 302. The commander-in-chief shall prescribe such rules, orders, and regulations, relative to the distribution of arms, ammunition, and military stores, to the militia when called into actual service, as he may deem proper.

§ 303. The command of any military force, called into service under the provisions of this title, shall devolve upon the senior officer of such force, unless otherwise specially ordered by the commander-in-chief.

OF THE MILITARY FUND OF THE STATE, AND APPROPRIATIONS FOR MILITARY PURPOSES.

§ 304. The moneys received from the several county treasurers, under the provisions of this act, shall be kept separate and apart from the current and ordinary finances of this State, and shall be applied to the purposes mentioned in this act and to no other.

§ 305. For the purchase of uniforms and equipments, pay of officers and privates, and other expenditures authorized by this act; the sum of three hundred thousand dollars is hereby appropriated from the moneys mentioned in the last preceding section, and from any other moneys in the treasury not otherwise appropriated.

MISCELLANEOUS PROVISIONS.

306. The commander-in-chief is hereby authorized to establish and prescribe such rules, regulations, forms, and precedents as he shall deem proper for the use and government of the military forces of the State, and to carry into full effect the provisions of this act. Such rules, regulations, forms, and precedents shall be published in orders by the adjutant-general, and, from time to time, distributed to the commissioned officers of the State.

§ 307. Whenever any non-commissioned officers, musician ,sor privates, of any uniform company or troop, shall have performed service in any such company or troop for the space of seven years from the time of his enlistment therein, properly uniformed according to the provisions of law, he shall be furnished, on application, by the commanding officer of such company or troop, with a certificate, duly setting forth such facts, which shall, for all purposes, be deemed *prima facie* evidence thereof.

§ 308. The commanding officer of every uniform company or troop shall, on the application of any commissioned, non-commissioned officer, musician, or private of his company, deliver to him a certificate, stating that such person is a member of his company, and whether he is uniformed according to law, and how recently he may have performed duty in said company. Such certificate, when dated within six months, shall be deemed for all purposes *prima facie* evidence of the matter therein stated.

§ 309. Every officer, non-commissioned officer, musician, and private of the uniformed militia of this State, who shall have provided himself with a uniform, arms, or accoutrements required by law or regulation, shall hold the same exempt from all suits, distresses, executions or sales for debts, or for the payment of taxes; and every mounted officer, and every member of a troop of cavalry or light artillery, who shall own a suitable horse necessary for his use as such officer or member, shall hold the same with the like exemption.

§ 310. The rules and regulations, prepared by a board of officers under section one of title nine of the militia law, passed April seventeen, eighteen hundred and fifty-four, with such changes and modifications as are provided in this act, having received the approval of the commander-in-chief, are hereby ratified and confirmed; and the commander-in-chief is hereby authorized to make such changes and alterations in said regulations, from time to time, as he may deem expedient.

§ 311. The commandants of regiments may appoint

ordnance sergeants as keepers of armories, not exceeding one to each armory, who shall be under the authority and hold office during the pleasure of the commandant; such ordnance sergeants shall be paid as now provided for keepers of armories.

§ 312. No person belonging to the military forces shall be arrested on any civil process while going to, remaining at, or returning from any place at which he may be required to attend for military duty.

§ 313. Any person who shall purchase, retain, or have in custody or possession without right any military property belonging to this State marked as or known to him to be such, and shall, after proper demand, refuse to deliver the same to any officer entitled to the possession thereof, shall be liable to an action for the recovery of the possession of such military property, and of a penalty of not less than ten nor more than one hundred dollars.

§ 314. Any person belonging to the military forces who shall, contrary to the lawful order of the proper officer, retain in his possession or control any military property of this State, shall be liable to an action to recover the possession thereof and to pay a fine of not less than ten, nor more than one hundred dollars, and shall also be deemed guilty of a misdemeanor; and any commanding officer may take possession thereof, or of such military property mentioned in the preceding section, wherever the same may be found.

§ 315. Actions to recover the possession of military property, and the amount of any fine or penalty under the two preceding sections, may be brought, by any officer entitled to the possession of such property, in any court of competent jurisdiction, and such fine or penalty, together with all other fines and penalties prescribed by this act, and by chapter three hundred and ninety-eight of the Session Laws of eighteen hundred and fifty-four, shall be paid to the treasurer of the county where the offender may reside, for the benefit of the military fund of the regiment located therein. The possession of any military property, or the amount of a fine or penalty, may be recovered in the same action. Proceedings at law shall not preclude the punishment of any military person in the military courts.

§ 316. Any person belonging to the military forces of this State, going to or returning from any parade, encampment, drill, or meeting, which he may be required by law to attend, shall, together with his conveyance and the military property of the State, be allowed to pass free through all toll-gates, over toll-bridges and ferries.

§ 317. Whenever any officer shall have served or shall hereafter serve continuously and honorably as commandant of any military company, under a military commission issued under the laws of this State, for the period of twenty years, the commander-in-chief shall have power to confer upon such officer the brevet or honorary rank of colonel, but such brevet shall not confer additional pay or emoluments for services under this act.

§ 318. All officers, non-commissioned officers, musicians, and privates of the national guard, while on duty or assembled therefor, pursuant to the order of the sheriff of any county, or the mayor of any city, in cases of riot, tumult, breach of peace, resistance to process, or whenever called upon in aid of the civil authorities, shall receive the compensation provided by the twenty-first section of the act entitled "An act to enforce the laws and preserve order," passed April fifteen, eighteen hundred and forty-five, and such compensation shall be audited, allowed and paid by the supervisors of the county where such service is rendered, and shall be a portion of the county charges of said county, to be levied and raised as other county charges are levied and raised.

§ 319. Chapter three hundred and ninety-eight of the Laws of eighteen hundred and fifty-four, except such parts of the same as are referred to in sections five and ten of this title, chapters two hundred and sixty-one and five hundred and thirty-six of the Laws of eighteen hundred and fifty-five, chapters one hundred and twenty-nine, and three hundred and forty-three of the Laws of eighteen hundred and fifty-eight, and all other acts and parts of acts conflicting with this act are hereby repealed; but such repeal shall not affect any legal proceedings commenced under them.

§ 320. This act shall take effect immediately.

ADDENDA

TO THE

MILITARY CODE

OF THE

State of New York,

PUBLISHED IN 1866.

GENERAL HEADQUARTERS — STATE OF NEW YORK.

ADJUTANT-GENERAL'S OFFICE,
ALBANY, *April* 23, 1867.

The following amendments to the Military Code, passed by the Legislature of 1867, are hereby published for the information and guidance of the members of the National Guard, and all others interested in their execution.

By order of the Commander-in-Chief.

S. E. MARVIN,
Adjutant-General.

CHAP. 502.

AN ACT to amend an act entitled "An Act to provide for the enrollment of the Militia, the organization and discipline of the National Guard of the State of New York, and for the public defense," passed April 23, 1862, designated as the Military Code of the State of New York. Passed April 22, 1867; by a two-thirds vote.

The People of the State of New York, represented in Senate and Assembly, do enact as follows:

§ 1. Subdivision two of section one, sections four, eight, nine, ten, eleven, twelve, thirteen, fourteen, fifteen, eighteen, twenty-six, thirty, one hundred and two, one hundred and twenty-one, one hundred and twenty-six, one hundred and twenty-seven, one hundred and thirty-eight, one hundred and thirty-nine, one hundred and forty, one hundred and forty-two, one hundred and forty-six, and two hundred and eighteen, of chapter four hundred and seventy-seven, of the laws of eighteen hundred and sixty-two, designated as the military code of the State of New York, are hereby amended so as to read as follows:

§ 2. Persons who have been or hereafter shall be regularly and honorably discharged from the regular or volunteer army or navy of the United States, in consequence of the performance of military duty, in pursuance of any law of this State, and such firemen as are now exempted by law.

§ 4. Under the direction and superintendence of the commander-in-chief, all persons liable to military duty in this State, who are not already members of the organized militia, shall be annually enrolled in such manner, and under such rules and regulations as the commander-in-chief may from time to time prescribe, and by and under the direction of such officers as he may appoint; but no person shall be so appointed who is not an officer or member of the national guard and amenable to military law for any neglect or dereliction in the discharge of such duty. Such enrollment shall distinctly specify the names and residences of the persons enrolled, and shall divide the same into two classes, the persons between the ages of eighteen and thirty years to constitute the first class, and the persons between the ages of thirty and forty-five years to constitute the second class; but the erroneous classification of any person liable to do military duty shall not relieve him from any of the penalties prescribed by law for non-performance of such duty. Such enrollment shall be made and completed in each year on or before the first day of July. The officer making such enrollment shall, at the time of making the same, serve upon each person enrolled a notice, by delivering the same personally, or by leaving it with some person of suitable age and discretion, at his place of residence, that he is enrolled as liable to military duty, and that if he claims that he is for any reason exempt from military duty, he must, on or before the fifteenth day of August then next ensuing, file a written statement of such exemption, verified by affidavit, at the headquarters of such enrolling officer, to be designated in such notice; but it shall not be necessary to serve such notice upon any person so enrolled, whose name has been entered upon any previous enrollment in the same company district.

§ 8. The commander-in-chief shall cause to be published once a week for four weeks previous to the first day of August, in the newspaper designated in accordance with law as the State paper, a notice that the enrollment of persons liable to military duty in the State has been completed, and which notice shall also specify that any person who claims that he is for any reason exempt from military duty shall, on or before the fifteenth day of August then next ensuing, file a written statement of such exemption, verified by affidavit, with the enrolling officer of his district, or the commandant of the company or regimental district in which such person may reside; and a copy of such notice, designating the places where exemptions may be filed, shall, for the same period, be posted by each enrolling officer in some conspicuous place in his district; and publication of either of such notices shall be a sufficient notice of such enrollment to all persons named therein; the affidavit required by this section may be made before the enrolling officer or commandant of the district, who shall make no charge therefor.

§ 9. Such enrolling officer shall not include in said enrollment, the names of any officers or members of the uniformed militia of this State, nor of the officers or members of any fire company, and the foreman of every fire company in any city, village, or town, shall, before the fifteenth day of May in each year, file with such enrolling officer of the district in which such fire company may be located, a list containing the names of all persons belonging to their respective companies, which list shall show the town or ward in which each member of such company resides.

§ 10. All persons claiming exemptions shall file a written statement of the same, verified by affidavit, with the enrolling officer of the district in which such person may reside, on or before the fifteenth day of August, in default of which, such person shall lose benefit of such exemption, except such as are especially exempt by act of congress. The captain, commandant, or other officer making such enrollment, shall thereupon, if such person be exempt according to law, mark the word "exempt" opposite the name of each person presenting such exemption; and if such exemption be permanent, the name of such person shall not be included in any subsequent enrollment. If any person shall swear falsely in such affidavit, he shall be guilty of perjury.

§ 11. The persons thus enrolled shall form the reserve militia of the State of New York; those between the ages of eighteen and thirty years shall constitute the reserve of the first class, and those between the ages of thirty and forty-five years shall constitute the reserve of the second class.

§ 12. Any member of the reserve militia may commute for the military duty, and for the arms and accoutrements required by law, by the payment in each year of the sum of one dollar, which commutation shall be paid between the first day of July and the fifteenth day of August, to the collector or receiver of taxes in the town or ward in which such person may reside, for which payment the said collector or receiver shall give his receipt in such form as the commander-in-chief may prescribe ; and moneys collected shall, by the collector or receiver, be paid over to the treasurer of the county, to the credit of the military fund of the State, on or before the first day of September ; at which time the collector or receiver shall transmit a roll of such persons as shall have paid such commutation to the commandant of the brigade district, except in the counties of New York and Richmond, where such rolls shall be transmitted to the commandant of the division ; and the correctness of such rolls shall be verified by such collector or receiver. But no commutation paid under this section shall relieve any person liable to military duty from such duty in case of insurrection or invasion, or imminent danger thereof. Said collector or receiver of taxes shall on or before the first day of July in each year, execute and deliver a bond in like manner as other bonds are executed and delivered by such collector or receiver, that he will faithfully pay over all moneys and perform all duties in respect thereto required by law.

§ 13. The reserve militia of the first and second classes, except such as shall have paid commutation, as provided in the preceding section, shall assemble at their several company districts, armed and equipped as provided by law, for parade and inspection on the first Monday in September in each year, at such hour and place as the captain or commandant shall designate in orders, to be posted in three public places in said company district for ten days, and shall be under the orders of the captain or commandant of said district ; and such captain or commandant shall make a register of all such as shall attend such parade, armed and equipped as aforesaid, and shall transmit a duly certified copy of such register, on or before the fifteenth day of September, to the commandant of the brigade, except in the counties of New York and Richmond, where such register shall be transmitted to the commandant of the division, but in all cases such registers shall be transmitted through the intermediate commanders. And in any county which has not been divided into company districts, and in which there are no officers to comply with the above provisions, the commandant of the brigade shall designate some capable officer from his command to attend to all the requirements above named. And in any locality where there is no brigade organization, the division commander shall in like manner detail a suitable officer from his command for the performance of these duties. The officer performing this labor may, in the discretion of the commander-in-chief, receive such pay for the same as is provided in section one hundred and seventy-four, military code.

§ 14. All persons who shall neglect to attend such parade, and who shall have omitted to pay the commutation therefor, as provided by section twelve of this act, shall be reported as delinquents, and shall be liable to a fine of three dollars. The several brigade commanders shall, with the approval of the commanders of their respective divisions, appoint in each regimental district one or more officers, before whom such delinquents shall be cited to appear, by order of the brigadier-general, on the first Tuesday after the first Monday in October ; and such officers so appointed, shall have power, under the regulations of the commander-in-chief, to determine the facts of such delinquency, and if such delinquents shall not prove their exemption by commutation or otherwise, as provided by law, the officer so appointed shall have power to impose a fine, as above provided, which shall be collected in the same manner as fines and penalties imposed by military courts are now collected, all the provisions of law concerning which shall apply to the fines contemplated in this section. And the officer so appointed to determine such delinquencies, shall have the same powers, and be subject to the same regulations as are imposed on the presidents of courts-martial, as provided by section two hundred and five of this act; and any such officer who shall be guilty of disobedience of orders, or neglect of or malpractices in such duty, shall be liable to the penalties imposed by section two hundred and sixteen of this act.

§ 15. The officer appointed to determine delinquencies shall, immediately after the performance of such duty, report his proceedings to the commander of the brigade, and the marshal or other officer who shall collect such fines shall pay the same to the county treasurer, to the credit of the military fund of the State. The county treasurer of each county shall, on the first days of February and October, in each year, remit to the comptroller of the State all moneys received by him and in his hands, credited to the military fund of the State, which moneys shall be kept distinct from other funds in his possession.

§ 18. The commander-in-chief shall issue such orders and regulations, and cause to be provided such books, and blank forms and returns, as may be necessary to secure the enrollment, and the collection of commutation moneys and fines and penalties as herein provided; and there shall be allowed to the military officers ordered on duty, in making such enrollment and collecting such fines, a reasonable compensation, not exceeding the rates allowed by section one hundred and seventy-four of this act, except that officers below the rank of captain may receive the compensation allowed to officers of that rank; which compensation shall be fixed by the commander-in-chief, and under his orders paid by the paymaster-general. The treasurer of any city or county to whom any commutation money or fines shall be paid, may retain therefrom one per cent as his fees for receipt and care of the same; and all collectors or receivers of taxes shall be entitled to add to and collect five cents as fees from each person paying such commutation.

§ 26. Company officers shall use their best efforts to obtain sufficient volunteers to raise their respective companies to the number of at least forty-five non-commissioned officers and privates, which number is hereby fixed as the minimum, and one hundred as the maximum organization.

§ 30. Each division shall consist of not less than two brigades, each brigade not less than two regiments, each regiment not less than eight battalion companies of forty-five non-commissioned officers and privates. Whenever any company shall fall below the number of forty-five non-commissioned officers and privates, such company may be consolidated or disbanded; and whenever any regimental organization shall fall below the number of eight battalion companies, or an aggregate force of three hundred and sixty non-commissioned officers and privates, such regiment shall thereupon be designated as a battalion, but shall retain its regimental number, unless such battalion shall be consolidated or disbanded.

§ 102. In the department of the commissary-general of subsistence there shall be a commissary-general of subsistence, with the rank of brigadier-general, and such commissaries of subsistence as may be otherwise provided by law.

§ 121. In case such armory shall not be erected or rented by the supervisors for the use of such company, the commandant of the regiment, in his discretion, with the approval of the inspector-general, may rent or erect a room or building, to be used for the purpose of such armory, and the amount of rent thereof, provided the same shall not exceed the sum of two hundred and fifty dollars for each company, in the several cities of this State, and one hundred and fifty dollars for companies not located in cities, shall be a county charge, and shall be paid by such supervisors, and levied and raised as hereinbefore provided.

§ 126. The commanding officer of each regiment or battalion, shall appoint a suitable person to take charge of the armory, armories, or place of deposit of his regiment, or of the several companies in his regiment, and all arms, equipments, and other property of the State therein deposited, and to discharge all duties connected therewith, as shall be from time to time prescribed by the commanding officer.

§ 127. Such person so appointed, shall receive a compensation of one dollar and fifty cents per day, for the time actually employed in cleaning guns, and other duties indispensably necessary for the safe keeping and preservation of such property committed to his charge, which shall be a county charge upon the county in which said armory is situated, and audited and paid in the same manner as other county charges.

§ 138. For the purpose of warning the non-commissioned officers, musicians, and privates, to any parade, encampment, or place of rendezvous, the commandant of each company may appoint a suitable person a warning officer, who shall be compensated from the funds of the company, and the commandant of each company shall issue his orders under his hand, to his warning officer or to his non-commissioned officers, requiring them to warn all the non-commissioned officers, musicians, and privates of his company to appear at such parade, encampment, or place of rendezvous, armed and equipped according to law and regulation.

§ 139. Each non-commissioned or warning officer, to whom such order shall be directed, shall warn every person whom he shall be therein required to warn, by reading the orders, or stating the substance thereof in the hearing of such person; or in case of his absence by leaving a notice thereof at his usual place of abode or business, with some person of suitable age and discretion, or by sending the same to him by mail, directed to him at the post-office nearest his place of residence.

§ 140. Such non-commissioned or warning officer shall make a return to his commandant, in which he shall state the names of all persons by him warned, and the manner of warning them respectively, and shall make oath to the truth of such return, which oath shall be administered by the commandant, and certified by him on the warrant or return.

§ 142. The return of such non-commissioned or warning officer, so sworn to and certified, shall be as good evidence, on the trial of any person returned as a delinquent, of the facts therein stated, as if such officer had testified to the same before the court-martial on such trial.

§ 146. Every non-commissioned officer, musician, or private of the national guard of this State, shall be holden to do duty therein for the term of seven years from his enlistment, unless disability after enlistment shall incapacitate him to perform such duty, or he shall be regularly discharged by the commandant of his regiment; all general and staff officers, all field officers, all commissioned and non-commissioned officers, musicians, and privates, of the organized national guard of this State, shall be exempt from jury duty during the time they shall perform military duty, and shall be entitled to a deduction in the assessment of their real and personal property, to the amount of five hundred dollars each, except cavalrymen, artillerymen, and mounted officers who shall be entitled to a deduction of one thousand dollars on all classes of taxes. And every person who shall have so served seven years, and shall have been honorably discharged as required by this section, shall forever after, as long as he remains a citizen of this State, be exempt from jury duty. No non-commissioned officer, musician, or private, in the national guard shall be discharged from service, except for physical disability or expiration of term of service. Discharges for physical disability shall be given only upon the certificate of the regimental surgeon; and no member of any company shall be discharged from service except upon the certificate of the commanding officer of his company, that such member has turned over or satisfactorily accounted for all property issued to and charged to him. Commanding officers of regiments shall make returns through intermediate officers, to the adjutant-general, on the first day of January and July in each year, of all discharges granted by them during the previous six months, giving names and grades of the persons so discharged, and the causes for which discharged.

§ 218. Subdivision 1. Every non-commissioned officer, musician, and private, for non-appearance, when duly warned or summoned, at a company parade, a fine of two dollars for each day; at a regiment or battalion parade, or encampment, not less than three or more than six dollars for each day; and at a place of rendezvous, when called into actual service, a sum not exceeding twelve months' pay, nor less than one month's pay.

§ 2. The commander-in-chief shall appoint and commission brigadier-generals of brigades in the several divisions of the State, except the first and second, whenever vacancies exist, or whenever they may occur.

§ 3. The staffs of divisions, brigades, and regiments, shall be constituted and appointed as follows: to each division, an assistant adjutant-general, with the rank of colonel, to be chief of staff; a division inspector, with the rank of colonel; a division engineer, with the rank of colonel; a division judge-advocate, with the rank of colonel; a division surgeon, with the rank of colonel; an ordnance officer, with the rank of a lieutenant-colonel; a quartermaster, with the rank of lieutenant-colonel; a commissary of subsistence, with the rank of lieutenant-colonel; two aides-de-camp, with the rank of major; and one aide-de-camp, with the rank of captain; all of whom shall be commissioned by the commander-in-chief, upon appointment by the major-general commanding the division. To each brigade, an assistant adjutant-general, with the rank of major, to be chief of staff; an inspector, with the rank of major; an engineer, with the rank of major; a judge-advocate, with the rank of major; a surgeon, with the rank of major;

an ordnance officer, with the rank of captain ; a quartermaster, with the rank of captain ; a commissary of subsistence, with the rank of captain ; one aide-de-camp, with the rank of captain, and one aide-de-camp, with the rank of first lieutenant, all of whom shall be commissioned by the commander-in-chief, upon election or the appointment of the brigadier-general commanding the brigade. To each regiment, an adjutant with the rank of first lieutenant ; a quartermaster, with the rank of first lieutenant ; a commissary of subsistence, with the rank of first lieutenant ; a surgeon, with the rank of major ; an assistant surgeon, with the rank of first lieutenant ; and a chaplain, with the rank of captain, all of whom shall be commissioned by the commander-in-chief, upon the recommendation of the colonel commanding the regiment ; but regimental staff officers shall not be allowed to vote at any election of field officers.

§ 4. The commander-in-chief shall be empowered to prescribe and enforce such rules and regulations in regard to the disbursement and accounting for the regimental funds of the several regiments, as may by him be deemed necessary to secure a proper disposition of, and accountability for, such funds.

§ 5. Division, brigade, and special judge-advocates and presidents, and members of any court of inquiry or court-martial for the trial of officers, shall receive for such duty a sum equal to one day's pay for field duty, for each day he may be actually employed in said court, or engaged in the business thereof, or in traveling to and from the court, allowing thirty miles for a day's travel, the same to be paid upon the approval of the judge-advocate general, in the same manner as other military accounts.

§ 6. Division and brigade inspectors are hereby classified as belonging to the department of the inspector-general, and all reports heretofore required to be made to the adjutant-general shall be made to the inspector-general.

§ 7. The county treasurers of the several counties

MILITARY CODE. 205

shall, on or before the first day of June, 1867, remit to the comptroller of the State all moneys which may have been received in any year by them or their predecessors, to the credit of the militia fund, from the members of the reserve militia of the national guard, on account of fines, for not parading, in requirement of section thirteen, Military Code, or on account of any sums paid for exemption from the service demanded under said section. And any sum or sums of money received from the sources above mentioned shall be applied to military purposes, the same as other military funds are applied and paid.

§ 8. Such sections and parts of the military code as are inconsistent or conflict with this act, are hereby repealed.

§ 9. This act shall take effect immediately.

The following order contains information of great importance to every member of the National Guard :

GENERAL HEADQUARTERS STATE OF NEW YORK.

ADJUTANT GENERAL'S OFFICE, }
ALBANY, *July* 29, 1868. }

GENERAL ORDERS, }
No. 18. }

The organization of the National Guard is established as follows :

* * * * * *
* * * * * *

REGIMENTAL ORGANIZATION—INFANTRY.

I.—One Colonel, one Lieutenant-Colonel, one Major, one Adjutant, with rank of 1st Lieutenant, one Quartermaster, with rank of 1st Lieutenant ; one Commissary of Subsistence, with rank of 1st Lieutenant; one Surgeon, with rank of Major; one Assistant-Surgeon, with rank of 1st Lieutenant; one Chaplain, with rank of Captain; one Sergeant-Major, one Quartermaster-Sergeant, one Commissary-Sergeant, one Hospital Steward, two principal Musicians, ten Companies.

In addition to the Regimental Non-Commissioned Staff above provided, it shall be optional with the Regimental Commander to appoint two Sergeant Standard-bearers, as the same are now provided by law, but such officers can not be mustered into the service of the United States.

A Regimental Band, under command of a Leader, may also be enlisted.

COMPANY ORGANIZATION—INFANTRY.

One Captain, one 1st Lieutenant, one 2d Lieutenant, one 1st Sergeant, one Quartermaster-Sergeant, four Sergeants, eight Corporals, two Musicians, thirty to one hundred Privates.

It will be optional with Company Commandants to enroll one musician in addition to the two above stated, as the Military Code provides for three in each company, but only two can be mustered into the United States service; also, in case of muster into United States service, there will be allowed to each company two Artificers and one Wagoner.

II.—No officers in excess of those designated in these orders can be recognized.

III.—The enlistment of all members of the National Guard, as provided by General Orders, No. 23, of 1867, is strictly enjoined.

Minors must not be enlisted except with consent of parents or guardians.

The enlistment of aliens is prohibited. Foreigners who have declared on oath their intention to become citizens may be enrolled.

IV.—The attention of all officers and members of the National Guard is directed to the provisions of law that the term of service shall be seven years, and that discharges can be granted only for physical disability or expiration of term of service.

Surgeons will give certificates of disability only in cases where the causes are permanent, and disqualifying for active service.

V.—The payment of fines or penalties for absence from company meetings, drills, parades, and other assemblages, can not in any sense be considered as a commutation for the actual service required of the officers and members of the National Guard.

Whenever an officer or member shall have been absent from three consecutive meetings, drills, or parades, without rendering a satisfactory excuse for such absence, either on account of illness of self or members of his family, or unavoidable absence from home, in addition to all fines and penalties imposed for such absence, the time from the date of the first absence to the date when the delinquent shall again report for duty at a company meeting or drill, shall not be allowed upon his term of enlistment; and the Commandant of the company shall upon the descriptive books charge such time, giving dates, against such member, who will not be entitled to a discharge for expiration of term of service until he shall have made good the time so lost and deducted, and shall have actually served the full term required by law.

VI.—Delinquent members will be dropped from the rolls in manner as follows :

Whenever a member of any company shall have moved beyond the bounds of the State, or having been absent without leave and returned to and fined by sentence of court-martial, and such sentence can not be enforced on account of inability to fine such member, and such sentence having been promulgated at least three months prior to the annual inspection and muster, then the names of such persons shall not be borne in place upon the first muster-roll succeeding such absence or sentence of court-martial; but such names shall be entered after the alphabetical list of privates, and opposite their names in the column of remarks shall be entered: " Dropped (May 30), removed from State," or " dropped (Feb. 9), can not be found," as the case may be, and the date entered being that when the person last reported for duty. But no member shall be so dropped, except with the approval of the Commandant of the Regiment, to whom the Company Commandants shall, at least three weeks before the annual muster, report the names of persons liable to be dropped and the causes therefor, which report shall be returned with approval or disapproval within ten days after receipt.

VII.—Members so dropped from the rolls shall not be included in the aggregate strength of the company or regiment as "absent," or aggregate, "present and absent."

On muster-rolls succeeding the first roll after such persons are dropped, their names shall not appear at all except by order of the Commandant of the Regiment upon evidence that such members have voluntarily returned to duty and paid all fines and penalties due, or have been arrested and the sentence of court-martial enforced, and in such case their names shall be entered in place on the next rolls thereafter, and opposite them, in the column of remarks, shall be entered "dropped (May 30, 1867), taken up (April 11, 1868)." And similar entries shall be made on the company descriptive books at the time the order of the Commandant of the Regiment, directing the dropping or taking up, is received.

Members, when dropped, shall be estimated as a "loss," and when taken up, as a "gain."

VIII.—In addition to all fines and penalties imposed for absence, the term during which a person shall have been dropped from the rolls shall not be allowed upon his term of enlistment, but he shall serve such additional time as may be equal to the entire term during which he was dropped, in order to fulfill the conditions of his enlistment.

IX.—Members whose names are dropped from the rolls shall not be included in any company or regimental report or return of the strength of such company or regiment, but shall be separately reported as "dropped." Their names shall be continued on the descriptive books, with appropriate remarks, and they shall be considered as members of the National Guard to all intents and purposes, as provided by law, and subject to all liabilities as such.

The process of dropping from the rolls is not in any sense a discharge, nor does it afford any relief from service or condonation of offenses, but is to be considered simply as a purgation of the rolls by the temporary omission of recreant members, in order to avoid a fallacious exhibit of the available strength of the command.

X.—Commandants of regiments will be held responsible for the proper discharge of their duties, in approving the expulsion of members, under section 161 of the Military Code. Such expulsion should only be approved when founded upon general bad character, unfitting the possessor for association with gentlemen, or base misconduct, and in the latter case only when the offense can not be punished by action of a court-martial.

In all cases, the cause for expulsion shall be fully given by the Commandant of the regiment in the general orders approving such expulsion, and copies of all such orders shall be transmitted to the Adjutant-General.

XI.—Transfers of members from one company to another in the same regiment must be approved by the Commandants of each company and by the Commandant of the regiment. If the transfer be from regiment to regiment in the same brigade, the further approval of the Commandant of the brigade will be required.

If the transfer be made from brigade to brigade in

the same division, or from division to division, the additional approval of the Commandant of the division will be required.

XII.—In the transfer of men, the Commandant of the company from which transferred shall furnish to the Commandant of the company to which transferred a descriptive roll of the man or men transferred, which shall set forth the date of enlistment, and the place where and by whom; the date of muster into service, and place where and by whom mustered; the number of days lost by reason of being dropped from the rolls, or for inexcusable absence, and such other records as may have been entered upon the descriptive books, and which abstract shall be entered upon the descriptive books of the company to which such man or men may be transferred.

XIII.—Persons who have served the full term of enlistment, but voluntarily remain in service, are, when attentive and efficient, deserving of high regard for their unselfish devotion to the public interests; but when negligent and insubordinate, their example becomes doubly pernicious in its effects upon younger members, and they may be summarily discharged by the issue of a certificate of discharge for expiration of term of service by the Commandant of the regiment, and without application on their part, and which dismissal shall be published in regimental general orders.

XIV.—Vacancies in the position of Non-Commissioned Officers of companies shall occur only upon the expiration of term of service of the incumbent, his death or discharge for physical disability, his promotion or reduction to the ranks by the order of the Commanding Officer of the regiment, or by sentence of court-martial; and any company by-law limiting the tenure of office by Non-Commissioned Officers shall be void.

XV.—The Field Officers of each regiment shall constitute a Board, which may examine into and decide upon the qualifications of any person holding or elected to position as a company Non-Commissioned Officer, and if the decision of such Board shall be adverse, the Commanding Officer of the regiment shall revoke or refuse to issue a warrant to such person, and an election shall be ordered to fill the vacancy.

XVI.—The "*First Sergeant*" of each Company is the proper title of the Orderly-Sergeant, who may be appointed to the duty by the Captain, from any of the Sergeants in the company.

XVII.—Company Quartermaster-Sergeants will be appointed from each company by the Commandant of the regiment, upon the recommendation of the Company Commandant. They shall have charge of all property in the possession of the company not issued to the members, and shall keep an accurate account of all property whether issued to members or in store, and shall make such reports to the Regimental Quartermaster as he may require. They will sustain the same relations to companies as the Regimental Quartermaster-Sergeant to the regiment, and to whom they will be subordinate. They will be under the orders of the Company Commandant in regard to all property in possession of the company or its members, and subject to the same provisions of law and regulations as the other Sergeants. When necessary, they will also act as Company Commissary-Sergeants.

XVIII.—The following modifications and additions to the regulations regarding the chevrons of Non-Commissioned Officers, are hereby made:

For a Regimental Quartermaster-Sergeant—Three bars and a tie of three bars in silk.

For a Company Quartermaster-Sergeant—Three bars and a tie of one bar in worsted.

For a Hospital Steward—A half chevron of the following description, viz.: of emerald-green cloth, one and three-fourths inches wide, running obliquely downward from the outer to the inner seam of the sleeve, and at an angle of about thirty degrees with a horizontal, parallel to and one-eighth of an inch distant from both the upper and lower edge, an embroidery of yellow silk one-eighth of an inch wide, and in the centre a "caduceus" two inches long, embroidered also with yellow silk, the head toward the outer seam of the sleeve.

By order of the Commander-in-Chief.

Official.
S. E. MARVIN,
Adjutant-General.

B. MARTIN, *Act'g Ass't Adjutant-General.*

THE AMENDMENTT TO THE MILITIA LAW.

The Attorney-General has declared constitutional the amendment to the Militia Law, repealing the clause exempting members of the National Guard from taxation to the extent of $500, and directed the Assessors to proceed accordingly.

The law exempting military men from jury duty is also repealed.

THE EXEMPTION LAWS NOT REPEALED.

OPINION OF THE ATTORNEY-GENERAL.

The following opinion of the Attorney-General, in relation to exemptions from taxation of members of the National Guard, addressed to his Excellency Gov. Hoffman, is published by the Adjutant-General for the information of all concerned. The patriotic Senator from the Eighteenth District will please make a note of this :

"*Sir:*—The question submitted by recent communications from the Executive Department and Adjutant-General's Office, involving the inquiry whether certain exemptions from taxation of members of the National Guard are repealed, has been duly considered. By section 145, chapter 334, laws of 1864, these exemptions were somewhat enlarged from those declared by previous enactments.

"All officers, musicians, and privates of the military forces of the State were declared to be exempt from jury duty during the time they performed military service, and from the payment of highway taxes, not exceeding six days in any one year. Such persons not assessed for highway taxes were entitled to a deduction in the assessment of real or personal property to the amount of $500.

"Every person who served seven years, and was honorably discharged, was forever after, so long as he remained a citizen of the State, entitled to an exemption of six days highway taxes in each year ; and, if a resident of any city (where not liable for highway taxes), he was forever entitled to a deduction in the assessment of his real and personal property of $500. Section 146, chapter 612, laws of 1865, repealed all these exemptions, except from jury duty during the time such persons should perform military service.

"By section 146, chapter 502, laws of 1867, these exemptions were re-enacted and considerably extended. By this section all officers, musicians, and privates were exempt from jury duty during the time they performed military service. They were entitled to a deduction in the assessment of their real and personal property to the amount of $500, except that cavalrymen, artillerymen, and mounted officers were entitled to a deduction of $1,000 on all classes of taxes. It will be noticed that exemption from highway taxes, as such, is omitted in this provision; and that the exemption upon property is extended from $500 to $1,000 to cavalrymen, artillerymen, and mounted officers.

"The following is the provision incorporated in the general appropriation act, of the present year, which it is claimed repeals these exemptions: Section 146, chapter 334, laws of 1864, which exempts members of the National Guard from the payment of highway taxes, and which entitles them to a deduction in the assessment of real and personal property to the amount of $500. This attempted repeal, it is obvious, is directed at the wrong statute.

"At the time of its passage the members of the National Guard did not derive the exemptions from section 146, chapter 334, laws of 1864; but such exemptions were given by the provision contained in the law of 1867, above cited. It has been suggested that, although the wrong statute is named in the repealing clause, that there is enough in the reference to the subject-matter of the provision to effect the repeal. The subject-matter recited is as variant from the exemption declared by the law of 1867, as it is from the description of the statute. There is no exemption from highway taxes, as such, provided in the enactment of 1867. There is a six days' exemption declared in the act of 1864.

"The provision in the paragraph of the Appropriation

THE EXEMPTION LAWS NOT REPEALED. 215

Bill, which declares that section 146, chapter 334, laws of 1864, which exempts members of the National Guard from the payment of highway taxes, clearly identifies the provision of the section and chapter specified by the subject-matter referred to as the one intended to be repealed, as no such exemption is contained in the act of 1867. Again, this paragraph provides further, 'and which entitles them to a deduction in the assessment of real and personal property to the amount of $500 is hereby repealed.'

"By the act of 1864, the exemption of property allowed was fixed in all cases at $500. By the act of 1867, such exemption, when allowed, is fixed at $500 each, to all officers, musicians, and privates, except cavalrymen, artillerymen, and mounted officers, who were each entitled to an exemption of $1,000.

"From this comparison it is obvious that the subject-matter referred to is the exemptions contained in the act of 1864, and not those contained in the act of 1867. It is difficult to conceive of the reasons for repealing the lesser exemption to a portion of the members of the National Guard, which would not operate equally to influence the Legislature to repeal the greater exemption of $1,000 given by the act of 1867, to the other members.

"It follows that the above clause, in the Appropriation Bill of 1869, does not at all touch the exemptions declared by the law of 1867, but that the provisions of that statute remain in full force, because its language as to the number of the chapter of the law, and its reference to the subject-matter, is expressly confined to the act of 1864.

"It is suggested that the paragraph in question shows a clear intention in the Legislature to abolish these exemptions. If this had been their intention, why was not the repeal directed against the statute under which such exemptions were claimed? Exemptions from highway taxes were given by the act of 1864, which were not given by the law of 1867.

"The Legislature may have thought it prudent to repeal them, and also the exemption of the $500 of property, expressly, for greater certainty, although such exemptions had, in effect, been already repealed. If it is argued it was the intention of the Legislature to repeal these exemptions, the short answer is, it has not done so. (The People *vs.* Bell, 38, N. Y. Reports, p. 386.)

"It is a rule, fundamental and universal, in the construction of statutes, that a repeal by implication is not favored, and the earlier statute remains in force, unless the latter is manifestly inconsistent with it, or unless the latter act take some notice of the former, plainly indicating an intention to abrogate it, and that a construction which repeals another statute should be very clear, especially when the repeal is of a part of a statute, and it seriously mars the harmony of a system.

"I am of opinion that all the exemptions to members of the National Guard, declared by section 146, chapter 502, laws of 1867, still exist in full force and are unrepealed.

"State New York, Albany, July 22, 1869.

"M. B. CHAMPLAIN, *Attorney-General.*"

www.ingramcontent.com/pod-product-compliance
Lightning Source LLC
Chambersburg PA
CBHW021829230426
43669CB00008B/908